# CORPORATE HEALING

by Mary Riley, Ph.D.

Health Communications, Inc.
Deerfield Beach, Florida

Mary Riley, Ph.D.
Sebastopol, California

Library of Congress Cataloging-in-Publication Data

Rilcy, Mary.
    Corporate healing
by Mary Riley : edited by Dot Chleboun.
        p.    cm.
    Bibliography: p.
    ISBN 1-55874-058-9
    1. Organizational effectiveness.   2. Industrial productivity.
3. Psychology, Industrial.   4. Co-dependence (Psychology).
I. Chleboun, Dot.      II. Title.
HD58.9.R55   1990                                          89-15319
658.4'063—dc20                                             CIP

©1990 Mary Riley
ISBN 1-55874-058-9

Publisher: Health Communications, Inc.
            3201 S.W. 15th Street
            Deerfield Beach, Florida 33442

# Dedication

This book is dedicated to those who have made deep personal contributions to my work and to this book:

George, my husband, for focusing me on profit, gently and lovingly.

Mark, my son, for creating joy in my life.

Keith, my son, for being my favorite entrepreneur.

Brooke, my little daughter, for teaching me about love.

Bill Williams, for opening my mind.

Peter Drucker, for teaching me about management.

Linda, for showing me the spiritual path.

Ron, for setting me on my own path to recovery.

Eileen, for keeping my vision alive.

The Hudson High School Class of 1964 for giving me the confidence to write a book.

# Acknowledgments

My special thanks go to the many people who were the inspiration for and gave their time, energy and help of every sort to make this book possible.

Dot Chleboun was the powerful support who consistently organized, edited and produced all the logistics and details for the making of the book. Rich Noland generously donated his brilliant and original creation of strategic planning sessions to the chapter on healthy corporate planning and shared his mastery of healing corporations. Gene Thornton gave financial advice and analytical genius to keep the corporate profit perspective always alive and accurate; he kept the faith even though, perhaps, he did not agree at first with the principles expressed here.

I thank Marie Stilkind of Health Communications, who grasped the concept of the book in a single phone conversation.

For their help, I thank Shawn Riley, Margaret Ifkovics, Jahna Moore, S. Morgan Daly, Bob Pauley, Jim Morgan, Edith Conner of Health Communications and, for their precious input, the doctoral students at Golden Gate University.

# Contents

# Preface

This book was started in 1977 under the title, *Uncovering The Hidden Agenda*, to be co-authored by Mary Riley and Howard Finn, a Los Angeles councilman and newspaper columnist. The point of *Uncovering The Hidden Agenda* was to clarify the distinction between truth and simulation in the workplace.

Writing about the truth was easy. It was defined as "relating to the facts." Simulation was about pretending. The word "simulation" always carried with it a dishonest undertone. It intimated that people were being purposefully deceitful as they acted in certain professional ways, using formal manners, saying polite things. But in our work, it seemed more that people didn't consciously pretend for dishonest reasons. We, as a society, have developed patterns of simulation that are now automatic. One example is when we say, "Nice meeting you," — even when it isn't.

In 1976 Howard and I were on a tax increment financing committee for the downtown redevelopment of the City of Los Angeles. One member of the committee who was never prepared usually covered this by getting angry and arguing with other members about trivial matters. The truth was, he wasn't prepared: the simulation was that other members were at fault. This member did not consciously say, "I think

I'll kick in some simulation now." It was a habit. He didn't consciously decide to do it.

Howard was a representative of the truth in the world. No matter what people asked of him, they knew he could be counted on to speak — not through any politics, not hiding anything, not trying to convince but rather to convey the core of the pure truth within him. Howard miraculously reduced the anticipated two-year building process to six months, which was seen as an act of real public service.

The Mayor of Los Angeles often asked Howard's viewpoint before making decisions and Howard was called on to mediate among other council members issues that had previously seemed irreconcilable.

During this time, Howard kept collecting examples of truth versus simulation as he observed the truth having a powerful impact. With hundreds of examples, we pursued our work on the book.

In August of 1986 Howard died suddenly of an aneurism. His death compelled those of us who had the privilege of knowing him to carry on his work.

For two years following Howard's death, I had been grappling with a way to describe the impact of the truth versus simulation so that others could have the advantage of Howard's wisdom. It is the rarity of someone like Howard that leads me to believe that probably only 4% of our population live their lives out of the truth with no addictive clouds. If we know just one of these people in our lifetime, we know the difference.

As the use of the word "addiction" became better known in the late 1980s, it started to explain simulation. *The purpose of addiction is to buffer us from our feelings.* Addiction is a process or substance that leads us to be dishonest with ourselves and others. It is the one thing we are not willing to give up even though we would be much more productive if we did.

Suddenly the simulation examples had a more appropriate and realistic name — addictive behavior — because they were subconscious, not dishonest or on purpose. We could each see it in everyone else but not in ourselves.

Public awareness of addictive behavior has skyrocketed. There is hardly a person around who isn't familiar with addiction and its counterpart, co-dependency. This raised consciousness is such a powerful and positive statement about the potential of the human race to heal itself that it has again inspired me to write this book.

# Introduction

Profit both creates and is a measure of corporate health. Similarly, an individual's satisfaction in life can be, in large part, the result of working in a healthy corporation.

The United States of America now ranks only third among the nations of the world in productivity. A 1989 Gallup poll indicated that 70% of those surveyed found their satisfaction in life comes as a result of working, but only half of that 70% are satisfied with their current job.

What's going on here? Surely Americans are not purposely striving for less satisfaction in their work! Are they? We say — not intentionally. But there is a major increase in nonproductive addictive activities within our corporate walls. Addictiveness is rapidly increasing and profit is decreasing.

This book, however, is not about drugs or alcohol. The addiction we refer to is not one of substance abuse but rather about corporations that have lost sight of their purpose, are consumed by activities unrelated to the corporate goal — profit — and have moved away from the efficient production and sale of products and services.

In *Megatrends*, John Naisbitt says, "In our minds, at least, technology is always on the verge of liberating us from personal discipline and responsibility. Only it never does and it never will." Technology is not the solution; productive actions are. Technology can assist and support people who are committed to productive and profitable work. It cannot replace them.

We read every day about CEOs with planning horizons extending no further than the current quarterly earnings report. We see leveraged buy-outs used as a short term "solution" to slow growth and low productivity. Similarly, we hear nationally renowned addiction experts tell us that 96% of our population has subtly slipped into addictive, unproductive patterns.

The bad news, we know. The good news is that there are proven and tested avenues to corporate healing which can restore the United States to the number one spot in world-wide productivity.

A healing corporate environment provides the opportunity for both employer and employee to discover addictive patterns and initiate the recovery process leading to productive and profitable behavior on a daily basis.

# PART

# 1

# The Problem

# Corporate Sabotage

## Causes

We saw many different factors that brought us to this point but three major national causes kept recurring: (1) the Vietnam conflict, (2) the impact of high technology and (3) the vast increase in substance abuse.

## The Vietnam Era — Conflicting Goals

In the 1960s we were asked to support a battle over which our own nation was divided — to fight or not to fight. Whether it was making war-related items, being in the military, knowing someone in the war or being in denial about the war, everyone was affected by it.

Closure on a war is important. Nations can re-establish their positions and set new goals. Japan, after World War II, accepted its loss, rewrote its constitution to decrease its military might and decided instead to compete in the world of business. They have become Number One in Gross National

Product and in aiding third world countries. Our country, which won that war, subtly moved toward a posture of helping other countries while not addressing its own productivity needs. Some historians say the guilt felt by Americans as a result of the bombing of Hiroshima is what turned us into a helper (co-dependent) nation.

Vietnam, where the U.S. became engaged as part of our Help Other Countries movement, escalated into a full-fledged conflict. If we were trying to fight a war from a posture of our World War II guilt and saying we simply wanted to help small struggling countries, this could easily be considered co-dependent behavior — putting the needs of others before our own. It gave mixed messages to our citizens. Are we goal-directed, powerful, productive? Or have we become a national social work agency?

There was never closure on this question nor on the war, only a series of very strong emotional opinions on each side. This, along with other factors, set our nation up to become dysfunctional with regard to individual productivity and commitment to the goals of organizations.

One young soldier who went to Vietnam willingly with the hope of making a difference in the world, lost his arm the first month there. He has denied any feeling about it for 20 years but when he saw the movie *Platoon*, it broke through his emotional barriers. He saw that for 20 years he had worked against every organization that had employed him. He had resisted and undermined authority and had been extremely critical of management without ever knowing why. He did numb his painful feelings temporarily but they returned in the form of helpless anger which caused him to sabotage authority. This soldier became a success story who has healed his addictive behavior through the corporate structure. His earnings jumped from $2,500 per month to $10,000 per month within two years. He is, however, more the exception than the rule.

### High Tech Creates A Higher Demand For High Touch

In both *Megatrends* and *Reinventing The Corporation*, John Naisbitt reminds us that technology has its price. The more use of technology there is, the more we need to deal with people as human beings, to "touch" them by having more individual contact than in the past. Touch means respect, acknowledgment, recognition, trust and communication. But in most corporations, high touch did not grow to meet high tech — and understandably so. We are usually so totally absorbed in understanding and setting up new technology that we often don't have time to deal with the needs of people. Unmet needs, however, lead employees into sabotaging habits: gossip, resistance to growth, fear of change, wasted time, etc.

## Process Addiction As A Reaction
## To Drug And Alcohol Addiction

Probably the clearest explanation of this link between drug abuse and process addiction is demonstrated through the Adult Children of Alcoholics movement in our country. This nationally growing movement has several million members.

Children who had an alcoholic (or otherwise emotionally unavailable) parent took on certain roles to assure their own survival. One of these roles was protecting the alcoholic parent from the natural consequences of his or her actions. In doing so, the children became part of the family lie, e.g., "We are happy and normal."

In *The Self-Sabotage Syndrome*, Janet Woititz describes how these children, now adults, operate in the corporate world. They are quick to give up their own judgments, commitments and goals in favor of a noisier, more addictive person (tempers, tardiness, errors) whom they are trained to serve automatically, first, and to cover for. Corporate goals and personal goals take second or last place.

In *Critical Path*, Buckminster Fuller stated that he felt the only way humanity will make it on this planet is if each person takes responsibility for his own work, goals and judgments; we must never sell out our natural knowing.

The secretiveness of drug abuse is what tempts us to blank out the problem. When confronted, most substance abusers deny its use. If they admit it, they say they are quitting "next week." It often looks as though everyone is normal at work or in a meeting. That's the cover-up. People get so brilliant in their cover-up that it seems foolish to even suspect a problem. Consequently, nonabusers begin to think they are crazy when, in fact, they may be the only nonaddicted people in a work group. For their own survival, going unconscious is often the only way out, for when conscious, they see users; when they confront them, it is denied; when it is denied, they feel crazy again. So in reaction to a country of possibly 100 million drug abusers, it makes sense that 96% of the population has taken on addictive behaviors.

## Symptoms

The sabotaged corporation is one that has lost sight of its vision, goal or reason for being. Such a corporation is undermined by activities and energies placed in areas unrelated to the goal or the vision. These activities and energies are identified as addictive processes.

Some symptoms of a corporation afflicted with process addiction are:

1. The profit goal is kept a secret. Employees don't know how much profit the firm needs to make in a year.
2. Those who are in on the secret goal know that either it is missed every year or it is met but where the profit goes is kept secret.
3. The stated goal and mission (if any) are not reflected by our actions.
4. When we leave work at the end of the day, we feel uneasy, a little crazy and off-balance.
5. We think that our corporation is much worse than other corporations. No one would believe what goes on here.
6. Work that once was energizing and exciting now grinds us down so we spend the whole weekend recovering.

7. We do not look forward to going to work in the morning (or evening).
8. Our corporation has spent thousands, maybe millions, of dollars on consulting packages and, even with the best of analyses, there is no lasting change.
9. There is a basic denial throughout the organization about the addictive behavior it encourages.
10. We operate most often out of quadrant A and/or C of the Recognition Chart (see Appendix 1) in the kind of recognition we give.

Employees of corporations that foster process addiction get drawn into counterproductive behavior — "They are playing a game. They are playing at not playing a game. If I show them I see the game, I will be punished. I now also play the game of playing at not playing the game." (1)

An organization that fosters addiction is a closed system. It is closed to behavior different from the behavior of the addictive group. For example, an employee group obsessed with making one person a scapegoat will ignore information that can't be used as evidence against that person. People who insist on contradicting agreed-upon falsehoods will often be fired, ignored or transferred.

In an open system, by contrast, people accept negative information and try to correct problems. Open systems are conducive to extraordinary productivity and service. Complaints are welcomed and corrective measures are taken. Open systems are a key to excellent customer service.

In a typical organization, employees spend 75% of their day complaining or explaining. The complaining often focuses on another employee but can also spotlight the boss, the company as a whole, the company's customers and/or the company's policies. The explaining often focuses on why someone cannot meet or commit to deadlines or on what someone is doing wrong. We are reminded here of the well-known quote of Henry Ford II, "Don't complain; don't explain."

Getting agreement from others about their complaints and explanations is a temporary fix to compensate for the recognition employees are not getting. (2) But this fix soon becomes habit-forming.

An engineer, reflecting on his career, tells how 20 years earlier, he worked for a large engineering firm where everyone was obsessed with criticizing the boss. This period was the low point in the engineer's personal and professional life because he, too, became consumed by this boss's weakness. The engineer was weakened in his own work by this distraction.

Those accountable for profit and new technology may also develop obsessive behaviors but of a different sort. Both high tech leaders and CEOs, feeling the lack of support from employees and colleagues, become obsessed with their lone mission to generate profit. It becomes frustrating for them to listen to employees because of the 75% explaining/complaining factor. They feel they are the only ones who care about results. Yet in refusing to listen to employees and colleagues, they eliminate a crucial source of information and, as a result, may make disastrous mistakes.

The final symptoms of a corporation which has been sabotaged is usually the loss of profit and productivity that was possible but — "for some reason" — just wasn't reached. We believe symptoms of sabotage can be identified and corrected well before deadlines are missed and quality falls short.

## Process Addiction — A CPA's Story

Process addiction is addiction to counterproductive behavior. In *Healing The Shame That Binds You,* John Bradshaw claims that "addiction has become our national lifestyle (or rather death style)." He defines addiction as "a pathological relationship to any mood-altering experience that has life-damaging consequences." The addictiveness he describes includes both drug addiction and process addiction. The latter is an obsession with a process or behavior that is nonproductive.

As we first read Bradshaw's quote, we thought, *Process addictions such as workaholism, perfectionism, obsession with being right, addiction to control — these are not life-threatening compulsions, like drugs!* We resisted getting involved in all this talk about addiction. The word "addict" is harsh and condemning — we were interested in finding how to keep productivity alive and well — not in being social workers.

But the research of addictive organizations, processes and behaviors proved shocking. Statistics showed 96% of the population as having addictive or co-dependent behaviors. There was no way we could address the healing of corporate sabotage or subversion without confronting and resolving the individual addictive, nonproductive activities that are sabotaging corporate profit in the United States today.

The purpose of this book is to zero in on counterproductive behavior in the workplace and then present a tested cure.

Pete, a conscious process addict, provides us with a solution as played out in the corporate structure.

Pete Martin is a senior partner in an accounting firm. His high standards and keen eye for detail make him good at his job. His partner, Bill, is the "people" person in the firm; Pete is the perfectionist. Pete's perfectionist behavior was originally a key component in the success of the firm. Clients knew that if their taxes, profit and loss statements and balance sheets were done by Pete, they would be perfect. Pete required detailed working papers from all his accounting staff and reviewed their work meticulously.

As the firm grew, Pete and Bill hired more accountants. This meant theirs was no longer a family-size company in which everyone communicated on a daily basis. As the staff grew, so did the problems. Worst of all, net profits were shifting downward.

The firm decided to adopt the Professional Growth Plan (discussed later) as a tool to assure productive communication. In the Professional Growth Plan (PGP), employees are asked to request the nonmaterial things they need in order to succeed. In addition, managers use the PGP to indicate what they need from each employee to achieve company goals. Employees' and managers' comments are simplified, documented and then reviewed after 90 days.

Sally, an accountant who had been at the firm for four years, said on her PGP that what she wanted most was recognition. Pete's number one request of Sally was that she do a more thorough job on her working papers. Sally resisted working papers but since she was going to have her number one need met (recognition), she was willing to do the working papers for Pete.

Every 90 days a follow-up is done to substantiate whether or not both parties have kept their agreements. At the end of the first 90 days, Sally was asked if she had kept her agreement on the working papers. She checked yes. Did Pete keep his agreement to give recognition? She checked no. When asked why, she said, "He wrote all over my work telling me to do this and that differently but he never let me know if I did anything well."

Separately, Pete was asked if Sally had kept her agreement during the 90 days on thorough working papers? Yes. Did you give her recognition? Yes. Two yes answers from Pete, a yes and one no from Sally.

Pete was surprised to learn that Sally had checked no where he checked yes on giving her recognition because in his mind all his comments on her papers *were* recognition. In discussing their conflicting evaluation during a five-minute follow-up, Pete found out that Sally regarded his comments as negative and unsupportive — not as the acknowledgement she had requested. He eventually understood the distinction between recognition as he saw it (comments on her work) and the recognition she wanted. (*Let me know if I do something right.*)

Three other employees had also separately indicated recognition as the number one item they needed to make them more productive.

The formal/professional structure of the PGP follow-up helped Pete to understand Sally's request. But more important, Pete could see that he was depriving Sally as well as others around him of the recognition they needed and deserved.

Pete did begin to let people know when they did a good job but this remained a difficult task for him. He feared that giving recognition would lower standards. It is difficult for us to change a behavior we have repeated for years and years. Recovery does not mean we can change everything about ourselves but it does allow for a new awareness and understanding that can make a shift possible.

In Pete's case, the shift from addictive behavior to flexibility took place when Pete admitted the shortcomings of his perfectionism. He could now honestly admit that he was unwilling to bestow on employees the quality and quantity of recognition they required. That was not natural for him.

In counseling Pete discovered that for 17 years of his life his dad had set the standards. Then his father became an alcoholic and Pete suddenly had to set his own standards. As an adult child of an alcoholic, Pete took on more responsibilities than necessary and has been repeating the pattern ever since. He saw in counseling that obsession with high standards caused loneliness and distance.

He discovered that he did not have to throw away the virtue of perfectionism — high standards. Pete also realized that he didn't have to be everything to everybody. His job was to maintain high standards. This allowed him to ask his people-oriented partner, Bill, to handle recognition and reviews for the whole staff. Bill agreed. Bill then told Pete he needed him to keep on top of scheduling, working papers and maintaining high standards. He was relieved to have Pete's support in these areas.

At the peak of Pete's addictive activity, the firm was losing money. Six months after Pete raised his consciousness, the net profit had increased to 5% and a goal was set of 10% for the next six months.

Addictive/obsessive behavior is not only an employee issue, it's a corporate issue and a human issue. If people like Pete are willing to acknowledge the sabotage, we are all able to change. Corporations can provide the structure and support to transform sabotaging activities to productive activities.

## Co-dependency — A Lawyer's Story

In *Co-dependent No More,* Melody Beattie defines a co-dependent as one who has let another person's behavior affect him or her and who is obsessed with controlling that person's behavior. Many co-dependents start out with caution, commitment and compassion but, like process addiction, the activities lose their authenticity over time and become sabotaging.

The definition we will be using for *co-dependency* in the workplace is *becoming obsessed with the behavior of another person,* addicted to wanting to be liked and protecting others from uncomfortable feelings.

We see an example of this pattern in Rob, a successful trial attorney whose co-dependency helped his career.

Rob, a caring young man, began repressing his emotions in law school in order to numb his fear of failing. This served him well because he passed the bar exam the first time he took it. Later co-dependency began taking the place of his anguish in the victim/client relationship. Rob could avoid feeling his own unhappiness by expressing compassion for the victim/client in the courtroom. Juries loved the emotion Rob demonstrated and found in favor of his clients, based on Rob's intense representation.

Rob had the courage to look at the helplessness he had been feeling during the last five years in his personal life. He was able to acknowledge that the more fearful the client, the more involved he became in the case. Rob had been feeling job burnout for some time and didn't know why. When he discovered he had been vicariously feeling his own helplessness through his clients, meaning and compassion were restored to his work.

Rob is typical of many professionals whose co-dependency inadvertently perpetuates addictiveness in others. Their clients/patients are often addicted to a substance or an unhealthy process. The professional then becomes a co-dependent of the client/patient. Co-dependency in a professional capacity is feeling our own emotions vicariously through others.

If we avoid taking responsibility for our own emotions, we are almost certain to cause sabotage in the workplace.

### Exposing The Enemy

*"We have seen the enemy and it is us."* Pogo

Addictiveness must be experienced (felt) to be understood. It is a lot easier to point to Pete or Rob in the preceding sections of this chapter and talk about their addictive behaviors than it is to look at our own. Before we proceed to identify and solve process addiction in others, we must take time to consider a very crucial point.

Addictiveness cannot be understood intellectually only. When we are intellectual and point to the failings of others, we become a closed system. We use the weaknesses of others to deny our own feelings. A closed system does not see the truth. To understand addictive behaviors in others, we must understand our own truth. This creates a compassion that must be there for the correct information about others to be received.

At a meeting of Human Resource Development (HRD) trainees, one attendee stated, "My CEO talks to me one on one, all excited about participative management. Then the minute he is in a meeting with his managers, he takes all the control." Another attendee snapped, "Why can't he just let go and get his ego out of the way!"

That statement epitomized the lack of understanding that many HRD people have for the CEO. Later, we will observe a General Manager who would rather die than lose control — not because of an ego problem — but because of an addiction to control.

People who have not acknowledged their own addictive behaviors can often be found obsessively criticizing others.

Those in the HRD meeting who had experienced their own addictiveness understood the CEO's struggle and could offer solutions to it, solutions coming from understanding and offering viable procedures approached on a one-step-at-a-time basis.

In almost every corporation, we see Person A telling how bad Person B is. B tells of C's weaknesses. C reveals D's problems and D is obsessed with E. E is compulsively irritated with A — and back around the circle it goes. Addictiveness has pervaded our corporations in the form of pointing out everyone else's weaknesses. This helps us avoid the discomfort of seeing our own.

Before we go any further, we would like to say that for those of you who have experienced your own addictiveness or co-dependency, this book will be of great value. For those of you who have not yet experienced your own addictive behaviors, this book is not intended to provide a means or a basis on which to judge others or to point out their weaknesses.

As long as even one of us thinks we are not part of the problem of addictiveness, we are part of the problem. The 4% who are not in any addictive patterns do not know they are the 4%. The 40% who think they are the 4% are a major part of our national addictiveness problem.

One process addiction that blocks us from taking inventory of our own nonproductive/addictive behaviors is that of narcissism. The narcissistic behavior pattern obsesses on self-aggrandizement so as not to feel the pain of emptiness. (3) In self-talk and other self-esteem programs, honoring the self is very positive. Being addicted is not.

To raise our national consciousness, we must all take responsibility. **We have seen the enemy and it is us.** We must all look gently and with self-respect at our own lack of productivity. Learning from others is helpful; blaming others is detrimental.

Again perfectionism, control, compassion — used in moderation and with self-directedness — can be very productive and useful. But when these behaviors become blocks to feeling life's natural messages, they become a closed system and sabotage the corporation as well as ourselves.

## The Dollar Damage

The U.S. corporate debt increased by $700 billion between 1982 and 1988. Leveraged buy-outs, which led to the debt, are only a temporary solution to the lack of profits. The real issue of low productivity must still be faced. A $700 billion debt forces us to look at the financial impact of unproductive activities in the corporate world. These behaviors have been attributed to stress, mental illness and/or emotional disorders.

Stress is often caused when the truth is being revealed to a person's closed system. It begins when our denial system is being invaded. Mental illness and emotional disorders often have the same basis — two opposing realities. Pete, the CPA, for example, felt that positive recognition would destroy his high standards. High standards and recognition were two opposing realities for Pete.

Stress/addictive illnesses have been estimated to cost American business over $150 billion annually. This cost includes absenteeism, disability claims, health insurance, lost productivity and other related expenses. Executive stress alone has been estimated to cost $50 billion per year. The $700 billion corporate debt, an average rate of $116 billion per year, accumulated over a six-year period, could be eliminated in five years with the abolishment of $140 million of the $150 billion per year consumed in stress/addiction related activities.

### 6 x $116.60 billion = approx. $700 billion

If the annual $150 billion is reduced each year by $116.60 billion, this would leave $33.4 billion per year to pay for stress-related and addictive illnesses and bring our corporations back to solvency.

A national goal could be to reduce stress-related costs to $35 billion per year for the next five years and cancel the corporate debt.

According to L. John Mason, psychophysiologist and Chairman of the Institute for Stress Management and Education:

> It is standard business practice to have accountants perform an audit to help determine the financial health of the organization. Today's executives and tomorrow's managers must address the rapid acceleration of [mental] health costs and the development of new strategies to improve individual productivity and performance.

# 2

# Sabotage From Leadership

Whether one pictures process or substance addiction, a key person addict can be a very powerful cause of sabotage, by far the most difficult to confront and uncover because, as Schaef puts it in *Addictive Organizations*, "It's cunning, powerful and baffling."

In addition to confusing others, key person addicts isolate themselves from the normal feedback that other employees encounter. Addicts surround themselves with co-dependent managers/staff/friends who feed their addiction. The addiction is often to control. Those who confront the addict are quickly removed and often have no idea why. In this closed system only positive feedback is allowed, thus keeping the key person addict further isolated from normal employee information.

Our personal experience with key person addicts has shown that they are very intelligent and their intelligence holds others in awe and at a distance. Thus others hesitate to question or challenge the addict.

## A General Manager

John was the brilliant general manager of a *Fortune 500*
subsidiary. He graduated from West Point with honors. He
mastered vast quantities of information and had instant recall.
When he made a sale in China of specialized trucks, he knew
exactly how long delivery should take, complete to the last
truck out of the door. He repeatedly surprised us with his
ability to conceptualize all the phases of his manufacturing
plant. With his engineering background, along with 30 years
of business experience, 57-year-old John seemed the most
qualified person to manage this particular plant.

But there was one fateful flaw that sabotaged John's brilliant
leadership ability — he became obsessed with control. He
worked seven days a week and had clear, well-defined goals for
his plant. Work got his adrenaline going and since he was good
at control, people usually let him have his way. However, this
same workaholism alienated others when he consistently became locked into courses of action requiring immediacy. (1)

John's obsession took a toll on his marriage as well and
after 15 years, his wife divorced him. For the next five years,
John lived in an apartment right next to the plant and worked
even longer hours.

As long as he kept the goals of the company in mind,
everything seemed fine. But as his addiction to control grew
larger than his commitment to profit, things began to change.
John's managers began to complain to corporate headquarters
that his decisions were unsound and that he allowed no input
from his managers on the goals he set for them. John was
setting goals in isolation. The managers retaliated by sabotaging every deadline until they no longer acknowledged deadlines at all. Finally in a management seminar when the
managers were asked to write down project deadlines, not one
manager knew or was willing to write down a single deadline.
John's fixation on control had finally outdone his effectiveness.

John was moved to corporate headquarters where he
reported to a higher executive. He was no longer Number
One. He did not have control over his managers because
they were aware of his reputation as a dictator and rebelled

early on. Losing control over those around him was too much for him. It was like suddenly taking heroin away from an addict. The withdrawal was very painful, even lethal, but John was such a private person that he never told anyone how hard this loss of control was. It was only after intense investigation that we could see it.

Four months into his new job, John was mysteriously involved in a fatal auto accident. Those who knew him best believed he took his life. For John, living without absolute control was impossible, although he probably did not admit this to himself. Ten months after John's death, the manufacturing company was meeting 70% of its delivery dates. Under John's control, they were meeting none. Sadly, although John left behind clear, well-defined goals, his addiction to control alienated his staff, sabotaging the goals he himself established.

## A Nursery Owner/Engineer

The second example of a key person addict is Will. At age 50, Will became a partner in a major land-planning project with two other people. There was a chance to make $40 million in this project and Will let his successful engineering practice dwindle while he pursued it.

Will was a very intelligent man. He read one to two hours every day on highly scientific and technical subjects. People were often intimidated by his intelligence and his keen intuition.

Will has one flaw that has continued to undermine his success — he is addicted to good news and denies bad news, especially if the bad news means he might have made a mistake.

With the big land dream in front of him, Will took steps to keep the 300-acre development moving smoothly. One of the two other partners, Clint, had become a friend of Will's. The third partner, John, was to arrange the financing. Will had a gut feeling about John, plus evidence, that maybe John's plans were inconsistent with the successful financing of the project. He was often late, seemed preoccupied and smelled of liquor. Someone even warned Will that he should be somewhat dubious about John but Will characteristically denied the bad news.

Rather than face the possibility of bad news, Will used a technique he later identified as "clipping." Clipping is the moment one's mind clips off a feeling and, instead, creates its own positive reaction. The next time Will saw Clint, he did not tell Clint of his skepticism concerning John. Will did not want to upset Clint (co-dependency) and he did not want to feel his own fear of loss (process addiction). Thus Clint and Will went into full partnership with John.

In less than three months, John started to undermine the project and act illegally. This caused the three partners not only to lose the entire project but, in addition, burdened them with enormous debts attached to the property.

Will's clip when he had adverse news was not new. It was an everyday pattern he had developed to avoid feeling things and to keep a sunny outlook. In some cases this can be seen as an optimistic attitude. For Will, it had become an addiction.

During the court hearing to get the land back, Will denied all charges against himself and as a result, the facts against him grew in magnitude in the judge's mind. In an average court case, a person who is credible and honest admits a few mistakes. Will's clip obliterated all error on his part. This denial influenced the judge to rule against Will and to accuse him of conspiracy. Will was shocked. One aspect of addictive thinking is being shocked at its results.

With no engineering business left, the loss of his home and all net worth, the now 52-year-old Will moved 500 miles away to start anew. It took him eight years to pay off his debts. But rather than take responsibility for his part in the loss of the land, Will continued to blame John and filed the project away mentally as John's fault.

Years later, at age 60, successful once again, Will started a nursery business in South America. His expertise and optimistic projections enticed eight people to invest in his new venture.

The second spring season, Will visited the nursery and noticed (a) the roots were not expanding as much as usual, (b) the leaf color was lighter than expected, (c) there were not as many young tree starts as he expected and (d) some were dying from excess rain. The unconscious clip in Will's pattern, however, cancelled from his mind all four items of negative news. He returned to the investors and said, "The trees look great. They are growing fast but it sure has rained a lot."

The investors could see that money was running low and, based on Will's positive report, requested that shipments be made beginning the following month to fill orders already received. Will went to South America to help with the shipping. In a phone conversation with board members a week later, one member asked Will how many trees he had shipped. "None," replied Will, "we are planting lots of new seeds and trimming and spraying, etc." The board member was puzzled — hadn't Will heard their instructions to begin making shipments immediately? "Ship the trees!" instructed the board member. "Okay," said Will.

The investors were irate when the second week passed and Will had managed to ship only five trees. They felt deceived. How could Will have told them in April that everything was fine, in June that he was about to fill the orders, then suddenly tell them there were hardly any large trees? Will, of course, had no idea why the investors were disturbed.

Will's behavior shows us how damaging process addiction can be to a business. Each disaster becomes worse than the last if the key person never becomes aware of his addictive pattern of thinking.

If we use our profit and productivity results as guidelines, we can often see when we are acting addictively and when we are not. Nonaddictive behavior clearly leads to productiveness and profitability. Addictive behavior creates loss.

## When A Key Person Is The Co-dependent

The key person as co-dependent is the person in a leadership role who becomes obsessed with being liked, being "nice" and not upsetting anyone. When deadlines are due or work must be corrected, the key person is often immobilized at the thought of hurting anyone's feelings. Thus the quality of work, the volume of work and the deadline often take a back seat.

This behavior is de-motivating to productive employees because they see the deadlines they strive for and the quality they seek not being followed up by the CEO. So they, too, lose their motivation. As for the complaining and poorly producing employee, his behavior is encouraged. As long as he gets angry, tired, overworked, frustrated or hurt, he can keep the CEO from pressing him to meet production goals.

## A City Manager

Paul is the first and only city manager of a 15-year-old city. He has personally trained and developed most department heads.

The city is at the point of deciding whether to be a sub-standard freeway city or a high quality suburb. Paul wants to make it a high quality suburb and has been so directed by the city council. Now it is time to get the department heads committed to this goal.

At the next planning session, Paul told each department head about the new goal — to become a high quality suburb. This means keeping cars out of No Parking areas, having trash picked up on time, assuring that dogs are licensed, overseeing that common areas are well trimmed and cared for and making the building permit process expedient and conducive to new high quality growth and development. The department heads were asked to write examples of what and how to pass this on to their employees.

The first department head said he was concerned about one of his employees who was obese — he did not know how to get her to lose weight, let alone work harder and faster. During the entire meeting, his only questions and concerns were about how to help the obese employee.

The second department head said, "How can I ask anything more of my assistant? He is a super worker but always uptight. I know he will have a heart attack if I give him any more pressure. How do I tell someone to relax?"

The third department head was concerned about an employee who smoked. Like the other two, he wanted to help the person quit smoking before asking him to do more work.

All three department heads were exhibiting extreme co-dependent behavior. They sacrificed the goals of the department to "help" people with personal problems (addictions). This co-dependent behavior not only keeps the addictions of employees intact but ends up making it the goal of all the city directors to protect peoples' addictions rather than looking for new ways of improving service and becoming a first-rate city. This co-dependent behavior has sabotaged the chance of being a first class city and has trapped it into mediocrity.

Paul, the city manager, shrugged his shoulders as if to say, "What can I do?" Just as the department heads were more concerned with helping other addicts than with serving their community, Paul was giving up the goals of the city to avoid being the recipient of their anger.

Not once in the meeting did any manager acknowledge, let alone support, the successful operation of the city. Nor did Paul demand it of them. Paul had become a co-dependent to his managers' co-dependency of employee addiction. He wanted to be liked. The smoker, the obese person and the nervous person might get upset if the city were to expect more from them. Thus the addictions of the employees were now the key focus of the leaders; avoiding conflict was the unstated goal.

## A Manufacturing CEO

Company X set a goal to grow from $10 million to $100 million between 1988 and 1997. The goal was established by the three owners — Tim, who was also the president, and two absentee owners. Tim scheduled a goal-setting seminar for the managers, during which he would announce this new goal. Next, he would tell each of them what he or she would be expected to do to reach this goal. Tim seemed anxious as he read his speech to the managers.

One of the first goals to achieve was handling sales orders that were not being delivered. There was a long backlog and customers were complaining. Tim could not bring himself to terminate the ineffectual vice-president of manufacturing, who should have managed the backlog. Instead Tim was acting in his place. He became immersed in the day-to-day crises and could be seen carrying parts around the shop. He had become an expediter. No one was attending to corporate profit.

Tim was extremely personable. People in the plant were very fond of him. He was, however, in crisis in his own life. He worked far too many hours, smoked heavily and was mourning the illness of his only son, who had cancer.

The addictive process here was co-dependency. Even though Tim tried to take a stand for productivity, his reward system subtly kept rewarding those he liked and who liked him. For example, supervisors all took a supervisory training course which taught them to focus on a $100 million goal and see how their jobs related to that goal. At the end of the course, each supervisor was to give a speech about how he or she could increase profit. Three people were to grade the speeches — the professor, the vice-president and Tim. The vice-president and the professor both gave Mark the highest rating. Mark's speech was about organizing and planning for growth then monitoring the progress. Dave gave the second speech about making it through a crisis, like the time the company made 300 technical pieces in one day. He and Tim winked at each other, remembering that incident. Tim not only graded Dave's speech the highest but superseded the other two scores to give Dave the prize. Suffering and drama was being rewarded. Planning for growth was not.

When the professor confronted Tim with the discrepancy between his goal of $100 million growth and the friends he was currently rewarding, Tim became angry and walked out of the room. Later we found out that this professor was the fourth outside consultant engaged to resolve these problems but when it was time for Tim to take a stand for profitability in the face of upsetting employees, he discharged the consultant instead.

When faced with their own co-dependency, people often panic and deny the real reason for their actions. Upsetting people was too much for Tim to handle.

The subsequent effort to improve company profit involved an outrageous expenditure for a whole new technological system that Tim is relying on to take the company to $100 million.

This is a case where a CEO is relinquishing his responsibility for making a profit and hoping a computer will handle it. Rather than confront his own co-dependency, it is easier to buy more technology. This is not to say that new technology is without merit. However, if Tim's stand is to increase productivity to attain the goal of reaching ten times the current profit in ten years, the technology would be brought in to support that effort. But Tim's real stand is to avoid upsetting people. A corporation cannot reach its goal based on such a purpose.

# 3

# Sabotage From Support

Employees fill roles established to support the operations of a business. This support can include anything from answering phones to performing brain surgery. Our research has been ongoing for ten consecutive years and shows us that the number one thing employees need in exchange for their support is **respect**. Respect can mean money, time off for personal matters, being asked for input, recognition (see Appendix 8). The number one item that management needs from employees is support — more, better, bigger, faster.

When management fails to provide the respect that employees need, employees will often turn to a union, some unofficial employee group, their Personnel Department or a therapy group.

Unions were initially created to provide this respect by promoting the welfare and rights of its members. The original intention was win-win: if management will take care of employees' needs, employees will be more supportive; that is, they will work more, better, bigger, faster.

Sometimes, however, the union, employee group, Personnel Department or therapy group can be misused by employees with addictive behaviors as a way to mask or deny the conse-

quences of their nonproductive (addictive) behavior. In the
first example below, an addiction to being a victim became
the addictive pattern for a whole work group. Their actions
became vicious and sabotaged the goal of the very organization they were there to support.

## One Office Workers' Union

Unions were initially intended to protect and promote the
welfare and rights of its members. This representation was
originally focused on the material needs of its members. It
was a subtle way of getting for employees the respect and
recognition which were often unavailable from management.
Union doctrine usually states that company profit is a source
of higher pay to reward employees' work. Thus, the original
intention and best use of unions can enhance both company
profitability and employee respect needs.

Because of their purpose — promoting and protecting the
welfare and rights of employees — unions are sometimes
viewed by employees as a big brother who will protect them
from abuse and provide respect. For some employees, the
union does fill these needs and a healthy relationship for
respect and support exists. In other cases, the union may be
used to perpetuate unhealthy performance patterns within
the membership.

An example of the latter situation is the office workers'
union of a local company where in a five-year period, employees filed grievances for discrimination on the basis of
age, sex, race, sexual orientation and religion, hoping that
management would come around to their way of thinking
concerning fairness and proper job performance. Racial discrimination was charged by Asians, Blacks, Caucasians and
Hispanics; age discrimination was charged by people over 40
as well as under 21; sex discrimination was charged by both
men and women. The time used up by both the union representative and management to close these and other grievances averaged 20 to 30 hours per month.

Investigation of this wide array of grievances revealed that very few were legitimate. Having all categories of discrimination complaints made the statement that discrimination was not the real problem but rather an addiction to victimization. "Unfairness" grievances in issues other than discrimination were consistently rejected by the union itself.

The employee who filed the most grievances has never mastered her job in 15 years. She misses almost every deadline and chats with some customers at length about personal matters while others are waiting. The union had become a way for her and others to avoid dealing with their own ineffectiveness and to blame management. Management personnel changed many times over that period. The victimization process was too powerful and manager after manager left in frustration.

But the demand for respect backfired. The managers became so fearful of the next grievance that they tiptoed helplessly around employees. They had no support and thus could muster no respect in return. Perhaps the employees perceived some substitute for respect in knowing they had the power to sabotage management.

## A College Faculty

A college faculty formed an unofficial secret group to sabotage the college president and the administrators. One by one, the administrators would become scapegoats for all the ills of the faculty. First, it was the finance administrator, gossiped about for being gay. Employees petitioned against him and refused to do what he asked. He had a nervous illness and soon quit.

Next was the operations manager. She had been with the college for 20 years and was not growing in the job. She played favorites and rarely followed up on her instructions from the president. While her termination could have been normal, the maliciousness of the faculty caused her to take a disability leave for emotional disorders, after which she quit.

The president experienced extreme stress during this period, which manifested itself in an eating disorder, along with a tendency to overlook the problems. He set goals and wondered why they were never met. He had recently hired a new finance administrator, hoping to solve the school's budget problems.

Without his having much chance to build rapport, the faculty built a conspiracy against the newly hired finance manager. He was a strong leader, strict on details but poor on acknowledging people. Because he was black, the employees did not use racial discrimination as their grievance. Since he expressed no warmth toward either men or women, they couldn't claim sexual harassment or call him gay. Instead, they built an embezzlement case against him.

Victim of the worst sabotage was the operations manager. As a single man with no children, he devoted his evenings and weekends to the job, trying to give the faculty the respect they were not getting from other administrators. He listened to their needs, solved their problems, bought them things and put his job on the line to help them. Eventually the board, secretly convinced by two faculty members of this manager's ineffectiveness and of being too close to faculty, terminated him. He was so hurt by being backstabbed that he lost 30 pounds and began alcoholic drinking again after eight years of sobriety.

This employee group had become obsessed with destroying those in authority. Rather than face the pain in their own lives, they have chosen to be addicted to sabotaging management. Like any other fix, it continues to mushroom.

The members of the faculty who were a part of this lynch mob were so camouflaged that the president could not see the actual problem. That's the nature of sabotage from process addiction — it is very carefully protected and concealed.

There was one giveaway. One by one, each faculty member refused to be promoted to management. In other words, they were hooked on the process of undermining managers to relieve them of their own misery. The hook was most evident in their refusal to promote to positions that would positively affect the harmonious operation of the college. The president and the managers have become co-dependent on the silent anger of the faculty. The goals of quality education were rarely discussed.

## A Personnel Department

Information on addictiveness and co-dependency and their roles in sabotaging corporate profitability is so recent that few personnel and human resource managers can be expected to take full responsibility for single-handedly healing these behaviors. Yet, in more than a thousand corporations we have contacted in the past two to three years, 85% expect the problems to be handled by the human resources department.

Our experience in working with hundreds of companies is that many of their employee development efforts have ended at the "stuck in partial healing" phase. The CEO believes the company is doing something since they have human resource departments, seminars, training tapes, etc. But if these activities do not directly and consistently reflect back to profitability and to what each person can and is doing about profit and to what form of respect each employee needs, it is most likely operating on the illusion of healing. It is often easier to shift from addiction to production in a company with a CEO who can start fresh, to have a full four-stage profitable productive healing than to deal with a CEO and/or personnel manager who is stuck in the illusion that the company already has a program and hopes it will — or should — increase productivity, any day soon.

Recently we were asked to work with a high tech company on their compensation package. Their turnover was very high and the CEO assumed money was the problem — that is what most people stated in their exit interview. While we were in the lobby, we noticed on the wall the following sign:

### Our Ten Values

1. Believe in people.
2. Grow in self-esteem.
3. Promote a sense of achievement.
4. Help each other.
5. Have open communication.
6. Reserve the right to make mistakes.
7. Promote training and education.

8. Provide security in employment.
9. Properly insure.
10. Manage with goals (decentralize).

We asked the receptionist if these were the company's values, to which she replied, "They are supposed to be, but no one here pays any attention to them."

The personnel manager then appeared and took us back to his hidden office, where he spoke to us in hushed tones. He told us about the high rate of turnover and said he wanted a new salary package. We asked him about the exit interview questions, the training program, the recognition program, etc. and found, in fact, that no such programs were in effect. The reward for productiveness was the employees "got to keep their jobs." He whispered to us that the people around there were not that great anyway so turnover was not really a problem. But upper management wanted a new compensation package so he would get one.

We later interviewed two people who had left the company and one who was still employed there. All three complained of a CEO who was out of touch with the employees and of the lack of realistic goals by which to measure their work.

A month later, at Hewlett-Packard, we saw the exact same ten values posted. That's why they looked familiar — they were Hewlett-Packard's values and at Hewlett-Packard there was no mixed message. The goals did match the employer's actions on a much more consistent basis. The efforts at Hewlett-Packard were in line with their stated goals and values.

When the smaller company posted the ten values, it was insincere and a lie is at the very core of an addictive organization. Scott Peck, in *People of the Lie* (1), defines evil as pretending to help people when one is actually killing off their spirit. In this case, the personnel manager was making a show of having Hewlett-Packard values without really defining his own company's identity and direction, thereby subverting profitability. Corporate healing is far too expansive a task to be handled by the personnel department alone.

## A Franchisee

Art gives us another example of a support function turning to sabotage. As a franchisee, Art's major role was to support the franchisor. He had a new franchise with everything going for him profitwise — good location, high market share, an upward sales trend and promising projected profits.

Because of his personable nature, Art's employees all seemed to like and respect him. Missing from his organization were clearly defined goals and objectives. Rather than aim for clearly defined goals, Art preferred working things out through people.

Having been overweight most of his adult life, Art belonged to Overeaters Anonymous. He had his 12-Step Overeaters Anonymous facilitator come to the company once a week to assist in solving company problems, along with supporting Art in his program. The facilitator did not enforce an Overeaters Anonymous agenda on the group but did guide them through the basic 12-Step program used for all "Anonymous" groups (Alcoholics Anonymous, Al-Anon, Adult Children of Alcoholics, Gamblers Anonymous, Workaholics Anonymous, etc.) (See Appendix 2.)

For the first few months this was very effective. People were taking responsibility for their own feelings and actions and they were learning to communicate better with each other. Art liked it because he felt right at home and it validated his OA history. He continued to report to the franchisor that he was developing his managers and employees into a productive team.

At the end of three months, it was time for the new team to develop goals for the business and for themselves — work goals. But Art's co-dependent nature led him to remain in the comfort of the group therapy. Art was more concerned with group psychological seminars than with profitability. He said he was more concerned about profit but his actions proved otherwise.

When a person or group gets stuck in partial healing, as with Art's group, it is usually because there is no game plan, no four-phase format that says stage one is (12-Step) group sessions, stage two is goal-setting, stage three is deciding who does what to achieve these specific goals and stage four is creating ongoing abundance consistently (follow-up).

In a February 9, 1989 article in the *Wall Street Journal*, Peter Drucker, well-known author, professor and guru of management, blasted what he called psychological programs that have nothing to do with productivity and profit:

> Company-ordered psychological seminars are an invasion of privacy not justified by any company need. They are morally indefensible and bitterly resented . . .

Drucker emphasizes that it's all right to ask the employee to acquire new skills needed for performance of the job, for example, learning budgeting or people-skills when being promoted to a supervisory position. But, Drucker says, the employer does not have the right to attempt to change the employee's personality.

Psychologically oriented programs aimed at behavioral change that do not link consistently, immediately and directly to profit and productivity are futile. Corporate headquarters was shocked when it found that the expenses Art had incurred for team building had decreased rather than increased profitability.

Thus, there are four main sources of potentially sabotaging "support systems."

One is the union being used to support a victimization process and to cover for poor performance.

Two is a secret group of employees who are focused on punishing management rather than carrying out the goals of the corporation.

Three, there are mixed messages — what support staff say and what they do are often opposite and often involve a personnel function.

Four, there is the illusion of hope — hope that psychological programs will somehow increase profits. There is no specific plan for them to do so — it is just hoped that they will.

# PART

## 2

# The Solution

# Opening A Way For Solution

### Research

The Depression raised our nation's consciousness in dramatic ways about the value of work. It is not surprising that by 1940, research had begun on motivation in the workplace. Once the urgency of the Depression was lifted, what would be the next source of motivation and productivity?

Frederick Herzberg, in his famous 1941 *Harvard Business Review* article "One More Time: How to Motivate Employees," wrote that his research showed that recognition, challenge and achievement were three key motivators of employees. Then, winning World War II became the motivator. After Herzberg, little was done at a significant research level concerning people and productivity issues until the 1980s.

During 1979-80, this author, as part of a team assembled by Xerox Learning System's Systemix Division (XLS), conducted employee attitude surveys. We sent questionnaires to employees of corporations all over the country. Of the 120 questions asked in the survey, not only was the data from direct answers considered but an analysis was done which showed consistent patterns in the answers to questions related to productivity. For example, we never asked people if they wanted more money or more recognition; instead we asked them to rate the importance to them of certain activities compared with others. We based our conclusions on 20 answers per topic. The topics included were recognition, challenge, achievement, growth, security and supervision.

While Xerox analysts gathered a large research base, each participating organization was able to discover how it compared with others. For example, nearly all those surveyed complained about administrative paperwork, yet each company wanted to know if its employees complained more than others. For them, research offered an escape from dealing with employees' thoughts and emotions. Having employees' feelings described on a computer printout allowed the employers some distance from the employees. The data was therefore meaningless to the employers when they read the survey results.

XLS had one of the most highly developed employee attitude surveys of the early 1980s but that did not mean employers knew how to apply the information gained. There was a staff of seven Ph.D.s, three of whom were psychometricians (skilled in the psychology of test questions), to interpret the analysis and four were management specialists. A graphics staff was available to illustrate the survey results on colored graphs. XLS became one of the first companies to start talking about corporate culture.

The overwhelming conclusion of the XLS research is that the number one thing people believed would motivate them to be more productive was recognition. Similarly, the number one complaint of employees was inadequate performance appraisals. (Performance appraisals were seen as inadequate because they did not lead to sufficient recognition and appreciation.)

Over and over, as researchers pointed out, CEOs and managers responded to these findings, in effect, by saying, "We know. We already know this." Their main concern on the recognition side, justifiably so, was how to give appropriate recognition to employees who were *not* performing. Meanwhile, the employees held back on performance until they got some recognition or respect. No wonder that Rodney Dangerfield, standup comic, made such an impact with his "I don't get no respect" comedy routine.

So the research was showing that people wanted recognition and organizations wanted it to be earned. XLS wasn't the only research company coming up with these tendencies. Many other companies were getting the same results: (1) recognition, (2) challenge, (3) achievement, (4) growth, (5) security, (6) interesting work and (7) salary, in that order, as items that motivated employees to be productive in their work.

In March 1980, the author's new firm, Morgan Research and Innovations (MRI), acquired the rights to the Xerox Learning System's Systemix System. We then did a follow-up survey in California to see what organizations were doing about productivity. What triggered this follow-up survey was a January 1988, front-page article in the *Wall Street Journal* illustrating how General Motors had used a salary-bonus plan to increase productivity. We had to ask ourselves — What do people do with research data? Throw it in the trash? After contacting 100 organizations of all types and sizes, we published the following report in MRI's newsletter:

### California's Companies Use Seventh Best Solution

During the past five months, Morgan Research and Innovation telephone-surveyed 100 companies in the North Bay area, asking chief executive officers to describe how they increase productivity. Twenty-one percent refused to answer any questions. Only 11 percent reported using recognition, achievement and other non-material rewards.

Research since 1940, following Frederick Herzberg's work, shows that salary is not a motivator, as was shown on the Xerox Learning System survey. Yet 68% of the companies surveyed (and possibly as high as 89%) still use the seventh best solution — money. Why? Our opinion is that money is easier to give than recognition, challenge and feelings of achievement, security, growth and commitment, the top six motivators.

By 1989, our research, along with ten years of professional experience, had touched corporations in California, Oregon, Ohio, Washington, New York, Texas, Alaska, Montana, North Carolina and Colorado. We find now that recognition has gone from 11% to 29% in corporations all over the country as a method of effecting productivity.

Recognition means taking notice in some definite way. Corporations are finally taking active notice of employees and their work. However, over half of that recognition is unhealthy. Unhealthy recognition fosters addictive and co-dependent behavior, as in quadrant A of the Recognition Chart (Appendix 1). The corporation is becoming a center for discussion of and focus on unhealthy behaviors such as smoking, drinking and drug use. Recognition is given to employees' personal problems more often than to excellence in job performance. It is as if we do not know how to give recognition or know what recognition really is, as it relates to work.

To illustrate the distinction between healthy productive recognition and unhealthy unproductive recognition, we have designed the Recognition chart found in Appendix 1. It shows that recognition in its noblest form is related to the work at hand, not to any individual's personal problems. Whether positive or negative, healthy recognition is about the work. It is useful feedback. Quadrant C recognition is characteristic of the key person addict discussed earlier. Quadrant A recognition is typical for the key person co-dependent.

Healthy corporations are those that recognize on an ongoing basis the activities that lead to productivity.

Ray Johnson, Executive Vice President of Nordstroms, cites continual recognition of employees as the reason for Nordstroms' long-standing reputation for excellent customer service. Nordstroms recognizes those acts which produce profits.

In summary, productive corporations have a profit goal. The goal gives everyone a gauge by which to measure his work's productivity. Employees get feedback as to whether they are acting out a pointless routine or contributing to abundance.

Our courts show respect for the mentally healthy aspect of work; history honors the joy and meaning of work; research shows that recognition of a job well done is the number one motivator in our work force today. For these reasons, we have selected the corporation as the ideal place to simultaneously heal and benefit from the abundance of productive employers/employees.

## Corporate Health Defined

### Abundance

A corporation is a group of legally bound people (usually employers and employees) who perform activities designed to produce a profit. In the interest of making that profit, someone must guide and direct.

**While technology makes repetitive production possible, we must make it profitable.** A high quality printing/design company with German state-of-the-art four-color printing machines serves to illustrate this point. A recent job of printing 10,000 brochures was done twice with errors and required reruns both times. The machine produced 30,000 brochures but no profit because, by the third run, errors had made the job a losing one.

Productivity, then, takes on a special meaning in a corporate environment. The state-of-the-art German four-color printing machines were not productive when 30,000 brochures were produced — 20,000 had errors — and only the 10,000 originally ordered by the client were paid for. Productivity, as we use the term, refers only to production activities performed efficiently and profitably.

We focus on the corporation as a context for the healing of addictive behaviors because of the corporation's insistence on making a profit. Corporate cultures expose regimented activities that do not make a profit; employees get feedback about their work and can change direction when needed. Any resistance to making these necessary changes (e.g., proofreading camera-ready art for a brochure three times instead of once before printing) is an issue that the individuals involved must overcome. This is part of healing nonproductive behavior. A well-run corporation can not only help employees adapt to changes but can also help them heal their sabotaging behaviors. In this process employees may renew or discover their entrepreneurial productive spirit. With profit as the measure and the gauge, employees can recognize that corrections are based not on subjective judgments but rather on feedback from the marketplace.

*Productivity,* according to Webster's Dictionary, is *action that contributes to abundance.* We know from the printing company example that not all abundance is desirable — e.g., 20,000 useless four-color brochures create negative abundance, glut. But the corporate structure suggests a positive definition of abundance as a plentiful amount of products and services that generate profit.

Outside the office, we may all want abundance in different areas. We may, for example, want more peace or more sex or more joy or more money or more clients or more widgets or more touchdowns. In other words, we will never all, personally, apply the idea of abundance to the same objectives. However, in the workplace, we can all agree that we want our work to be productive, to make a difference to the customer and to provide profit for the company so the company can pay us for our work.

A further clarification of productivity in corporations was achieved in the January/February 1989 issue of the *Harvard Business Review.* Kenichi Ohmae, a Japanese author and specialist on business strategy, says, "Doing more better isn't always productive." What is productive, according to Ohmae, is the ability to look with fresh eyes. Such a strategy requires *torawarena sunao-na kokoro* (mind that does not stick). The opposite of a mind that does not stick is a mind that does stick — a mind caught up in addictive thinking.

A productive corporation is one whose leaders have open (unstuck) minds and fresh eyes. It creates abundance because someone pays attention to the outside world — to the marketplace which regulates abundance. Many corporations with open-minded leaders recognized technology as the source of abundance in the 1970s and '80s. In the '90s, healing unproductiveness and converting it to productivity will be a source of abundance.

In healthy corporations, top management keeps the focus on strategic planning, on where the company wants to be and how to get there. Their vision and strategy provide a vehicle for employee transformation within the corporate structure.

## Self-Respect

In a dissenting opinion in 1922, Justice Holmes made a very significant statement about the contribution of work to the population's mental health.

In *United States v. Mooreland,* 258 U.S. 433 425 Ct. 368, the jury ruled that Mooreland was to get the worst possible punishment other than death — life imprisonment with hard labor. As Justice Holmes reviewed the case, he apparently wrestled with the subject of solitary confinement versus manual labor. He decided that solitary confinement was a harsher punishment than hard labor. For in laboring, he believed, people feel a sense of accomplishment, satisfaction, challenge or productiveness. In contrast, he believed solitary confinement typically produces loneliness, frustration, anger and sadness.

> ". . . hard labor [can be a] means of restoring
> and giving self-respect." (1)

## Meaningful Work

In Will Durant's book, *Dual Autobiography,* he recalls his lifetime devotion to writing the *History of Civilization,* a series of world history books he co-authored with Ariel Durant. His account of a particular event in 1931 supports our view that work can be a healing element.

In 1931 there were many suicides in the United States as people lost their money in the stock market crash and felt the devastation of unemployment during the Great Depression. That year Ray Long, the well-known editor of *Cosmopolitan* magazine, asked Will Durant, well-known philosopher of the era, to write an article for the magazine. Long wanted Durant to

reveal what he believed to be the meaning of life, to help
people find the will to live instead of killing themselves.

Durant, instead of writing introspective essays, wanted to
write about what meaning other people found in life. He wrote
letters to Will Rogers, Sinclair Lewis, Eugene O'Neill, Bertrand
Russell, to a convict serving a life sentence and several senators
and congressmen. He asked them to take a moment from their
busy schedules to define the meaning of life; the results were
to be published in *Cosmopolitan*.

Letter after letter came back saying, There is no meaning —
I'm too busy — I don't know. Durant was then forced to
grapple with the subject himself and this is what he came up
with: "The secret of significance and content is to have a task
which consumes all one's energies, lifts the individual out of
himself and makes human life a little richer than before." (2)

If a meaningful task was Durant's solution to avoiding suicide
during the Great Depression, can we not also find it a solution
to addictiveness (avoiding pain) in our work today? Corporations can indeed promote healing of sabotaging behaviors in
this high technology era. To do this, corporations must create
meaningful and clear goals that are realistic and agreed upon.
Within that framework, as we will see later, employees begin
to find meaning in their tasks.

## Bridging The Gap

### When Push Comes To Shove

Bookstores and libraries are rapidly expanding their selec-
tions of books, tapes and periodicals on the topics of addiction
and co-dependency.

Books on addiction are usually on one side of the library or
bookstore under self-help, psychology, health, philosophy or
religion. On the other side is the business section, where books
on productivity, profitability, corporate life, work life are kept.
The two sections rarely adjoin.

In our review of the literature, there seemed to be a point at which the healing of people's addictions went too far. At the same time, books on corporations went too far in another direction. The literature on addiction had a consistent theme which seemed to blame the corporate world, society and, at times, the Caucasian male CEO, for addictive behavior in organizations. Much as we were impressed with some concepts in Schaef's *Addictive Organizations,* the constant use of women and minority viewpoints and the rare acknowledgement of any healthy male CEO flashed a red light. For example, she states, "It is in the interest of society to promote numbness and keep us zombie-like so we won't rebel at racism, nuclear war, pollution, etc." Who is this illusionary society that has been subtly cast as a stereotyped villain? This lack of empathy for corporate CEOs could shut the door on CEOs and corporation owners to hear Schaef's important message.

The same push is on the business side of the literature. Books and tapes describe goals and excellence, how to get there and specific calculated steps to profitability. One of the most common channels for individual and organizational productiveness in 1989 has been the popularity of motivational tapes. Most people we meet who are excited about goals in their organization are listening to these. In one such tape, Brian Tracy goes so far as to say, "There is no need for negative emotion." This comment has had a controversial effect on some listeners, particularly those who are aware of the 96% level of addictiveness pervading our society because of the urge to deny feelings. We are only recently discovering that just after healing negative feelings, there often appears the entrepreneurial spirit, productiveness, enthusiasm for goals, etc. The spirit of corporate healing is that which allows the views of both Schaef and Tracy to coexist, each without denying the other or making a villain of the other. It is this synthesis, discussed earlier, this merging and creating a new way, that we believe can allow the 1990s to be the era in which we shift from addiction to healthy production, the era in which two separate camps — one that focuses on the suffering of people, and one on the productiveness of people — will merge.

## Transcending Either/Or Thinking

In the past 20 to 30 years, there has been a major division between those who support U.S. corporations and those who oppose them. Both have their reasons. Probably an equal number of historians will record both sides. Whether the dichotomy is pro-war versus anti-war, money-oriented versus people-oriented, theory $x$ versus theory $y$, addiction versus co-dependency, fighting versus healing or environment versus development, we have created patterns of either/or thinking.

President Bush's 1989 inaugural address, in calling upon us to bridge these differences and become one strong and gentle nation, also calls upon us to transcend both sides of this division and open our minds to becoming one. Emotional healing and corporate productivity can be one and the same. We can create a strong and gentle corporation.

# 5

# Healing From The Core

### The 12-Step Program For The Workplace

The basic 12-Step Program (see Appendix 2) on which this is based has a proven record for dealing with addictions. "Perhaps the fastest growing spiritual movement in the world today is the 12-Step Program." (1)

Our first recommendation would be for as many people as possible to attend the most appropriate 12-Step Program they can. In the 12-Step Program For The Workplace and following (Appendix 3) we have made some changes that we believe will enhance corporate healing. We have referred to our spiritual side as the entrepreneurial spirit, the part of us that really wants to make a difference, to create, to be good in our work. (2)

Our experience has been that the gap between the spiritual steps to addiction recovery and the productivity goals of corporations needs to be bridged gently and with all due respect to both worlds. Our revising the basic 12-Steps does not imply that the 12-Step spiritual bent is wrong. We offer an alternative to corporations whose philosophy of productiveness fits better with an entrepreneurial spirit concept than a religious concept. It is an attempt to acknowledge the best of spiritual healing and the best of corporate structure. Our experience has shown us that they can enhance one another and renew entrepreneurial spirit.

"The entrepreneurial spirit has been squeezed out of most of us, yet this spirit is the core of our innovation and creativity." (3) Thus, we recommend going to the core of the injured entrepreneurial spirit and reviving it if it is numbed or repressed and redirecting it if it has become excessive or self-sabotaging.

### Step 1
**We admitted we were powerless over [whatever
the addiction] and our productiveness
has decreased because of it.**

When we blame everyone around us, the boss, the organization, our spouse, etc., we reduce the possibility of healing ourselves. As long as we say "One of these days, I'll get around to that"—"Someday, I'll get organized"—"Beginning next week, I'll do a better job"— we are nurturing our addictive behavior. We must accept that this is one behavior we cannot heal alone and be willing to accept support, guidance and assistance from others.

### Step 2
**We came to accept that we do not currently
know everything we could know about our jobs.**

One of the common games people play is "knowing everything." Many people speak and act on things they know little or nothing about but are unwilling to let anyone know they don't know.

I remember substitute teaching for a junior high school science class when a student was giving a presentation on a current event about a *rabid bat*. Not knowing what rabid meant and not willing to admit I didn't know, I heard it as *rabbit bat.* When a student asked "What is a rabid bat?" I said, all-knowingly, "It's half rabbit and half bat." Everyone accepted it. Many years later when I came across the word rabid, I was shocked to find I had given false information to 40 students.

As a trainer in the corporate world for ten years, I have seen how much employees resist being trained (the term "trainer" does have a dog-trainer ring to it). Somehow our resistance to learning has kept us all in less productive places in our lives.

Step 2 is a call to accept learning — to let go of the resistance to it — to accept that we do not already know everything and open our minds to learning new and productive things.

### Step 3
### We have made a decision to accept
### the guidance of others in the organization.

This can be a tough step to follow. One of our reviewers warned that there must be a caution — a guideline — for identifying health in a person because until we ourselves are healthy, we don't have the eyes to recognize someone who is. We might make a terrible mistake by trusting guidance from the wrong person. Our response is that this is why the corporation is the context, the environment, for healing addictive behavior. The choice of guidance is someone who has results — we see what he or she has built, healed, sold, organized, pulled off, balanced, predicted, etc. and, based on the results of the work, we choose what to learn from that person.

Step 3 means learning from those who have successful track records and could help us become more productive and satisfied in our work. We do not have to like that person. We just have to be open to learning something about the work which they know better than we do.

The corporate version of recovering from our addictions is seeking help to keep us on track on our jobs. There is plenty of excellent guidance available but only a few people are willing to learn. As mentioned earlier, many of us get stuck in

viewpoints that were productive at first but which later became destructive and addictive, without our noticing.

For example, one president of a financial corporation was
excellent at staying focused on financial profit goals. Bob was
so good he did not need much help at first. In fact, he had a
very difficult time trusting anyone. He was tightly holding to
the viewpoint that financial goals were always number one
and that people were often irritants taking him away from the
goals. He could do it alone!

In the Professional Growth Plan review between Bob and
his board of directors, they were asked to identify the number
one thing each wanted from the other. The number one item
the board wanted from Bob was that he "motivate and develop
his employees." This infuriated Bob. "Don't they care about
financial goals? This is the fastest growing financial institution
in this part of the state and all they care about is touchy-feely
stuff. I'd better get out of here fast. I'm in the wrong place."

Bob argued that money, not people, was the key. We agreed
to have him discuss it with the president of the board. They
argued for two hours. Bob was saying, "I thought increasing
profit was my job, not being a personnel person." The board
president was saying, "It is! You've done a great job. Keep it
up. Now, can we improve in one area: motivating and developing people?" "I already am!" said Bob.

Bob finally started to come around when we drew a GAP
diagram. There was a discrepancy (gap) between what he
was doing to develop his staff and what the board wanted
done. The board was the guidance in this case — they could
see he was a superstar. He was doing all the work but the
management team was weak and a potential problem.

We must have shown Bob the picture of the gap 25 times
over the next two weeks. We'd be on other topics and suddenly his anger would arise again. "I'm already doing a lot for
my employees." "Yes, Bob, you are. The board only wants a
few more actions to build strong managers."

But a timely life-changing event occurred. Bob was away at a
financial retreat when an inner voice told him to go home. He
did and there was his wife in his home with another man. She

had been telling him for years that he was ignoring her, spending such long hours at work but he hadn't wanted to hear her.

The evidence in Bob's universe finally got him to let go of his negative will (his addiction to being right and in control). He enrolled in therapy, first with his wife and then by himself. As a result he began to listen.

Bob eventually accepted the guidance of the board and it has transformed his life. He is developing his managers into more responsible team players so he can work a 40-hour week and spend more time at home. He and his wife went on a two-week cruise — in the previous five years he had never even taken a full week's vacation. It was win-win. But — had he been in the 12-Step program, he could have agreed and accepted the board's guidance without so much resistant energy loss. It was rare and lucky that there were enough people and events in his life to break through this resistance.

Step 3 is about agreeing to let our resistance down so we can be guided by others in the corporation to see things differently.

### Step 4
### We make a searching and fearless
### moral inventory of ourselves.

This step, like Steps 1 through 3, takes tremendous courage but the rewards are very high.

Most of us can blame negative events on people around us. This is usually rampant in the workplace.

In her second month working for a major corporation, Sue spoke up at a meeting concerning a problem and said she was partly responsible because of her own procrastination. No one else spoke up and the issue was considered filed — as Sue's problem. In addition, the next several similar problems were blamed on Sue. Since no one else took moral inventory or accepted responsibility, Sue, who was in a 12-Step program, was an easy target for blame. But when everyone takes responsibility for nonproductive activities and the

environment supports and encourages productivity and high
morale, it is much easier.

Step 4 is well expressed in *Home Away From Home* by
Janet G. Woititz, about ACoAs (Adult Children of Alcoholics)
in the workplace. The overwhelming feeling of most ACoAs,
behind all their defenses and unproductive behavior, is their
perceived inadequacy to do the job. If we can take a moral
inventory, even though it pinches, we can conquer the source
of the feeling of inadequacy.

## Step 5
### We admitted to ourselves and to another human being the exact nature of our sabotaging behavior on the job.

In *Healing The Shame That Binds You*, John Bradshaw
brilliantly describes healthy shame versus toxic shame. Healthy
shame gives us permission to be human, it tells us our limits
and lets us know we can and will make mistakes; it is the
psychological foundation for humility.

Toxic shame, says Bradshaw, is unbearable and always necessitates a cover-up, a false self. Toxic shame is at the core of most
emotional illness. This cover-up results in a lifetime of secrecy
and hiding — the basic cause of nonproductive behavior in the
corporate environment. The energy needed to keep up this
facade is so great that there is no energy left to be productive.

Step 5 tells us to find another person in recovery, probably
not on the job if it would threaten job security, to whom we
admit the nature of our unproductive behavior. For example,
Fran admitted that she had a habit of criticizing people. She
got a high from talking about the shortcomings of others. As
she told her friend, who was a good listener, she became
aware that she got a fix from the feeling of superiority she
experienced when she belittled others.

## Step 6
### We were entirely ready to listen
### to the guidance and, for a moment,
### let go of our original viewpoint.

In the case of Bob, the financial institution CEO, it looked to him as though letting go of his obsession with profit goals would destroy the corporation. That is why he needed to trust the guidance that came to him through the board. They might not be perfect but that does not preclude the possibility that they might see something we don't.

## Step 7
### Acknowledged the guidance. Summarized it.
### Asked questions to further understand it.
### Said thank you and agreed to undertake the suggestion.

Step 7 allows us to discover if our addictiveness may have closed us off. Openness to learning keeps us from being defensive and creates a positive rapport with others in the corporation who have some knowledge in an area where, perhaps, we do not.

Using Bob again as an example, he had a very difficult time acknowledging the value of the board's request that he motivate and develop his staff. Ron, who spoke for the board, had thought for a long time about the urgency of Bob's developing a strong management team. The issue had come up in the past on many occasions. In Bob's mind, however, acknowledging the suggestion of the board, an opinion he didn't agree with, would somehow cancel his viewpoint. The key here is that Bob's viewpoint will not be negated. Two points of view can be intact at the same time. "Yes, profit is number one. You did an excellent job of achieving profit," and, "Yes, a next step could be to develop staff." This is part of transcending either/ or thinking.

In order to prevent Bob's fear of inadequacy from emerging and causing him to fixate on his viewpoint, he needs to make a conscious decision to acknowledge guidance. If we are not going to allow ourselves to be guided by others in the organization, all our energy will go to resistance.

### Step 8
We made a list of all the persons we had harmed
and became willing to make amends to them,
to others or to the corporation.

### Step 9
We made direct amends to such people whenever
possible except when to do so would
injure them or others.

Much of Steps 8 and 9 are about the sudden realization we have — now that we see our addictive behavior — of how it has harmed others. It takes tremendous courage to look at the truth about ourselves but we must remember that it is the key that frees us in our work and releases our productive spirit.

Lee, a contractor, has an addictive perfectionism. Whenever he is on a project, he keeps nagging at the engineer, the architect and the workers to get this right, get that right and do it now — my way. Those who are in partnership with Lee on his buildings are very happy because they benefit from his perfectionism. But for those he nags, it takes its toll. One engineer was a kind and gentle man named Jon. Jon was an excellent civil engineer, committed to doing a good job for the client and to keeping him happy. During one project, Lee was working right next to Jon's office on another project. Several times a day, Lee would rush to Jon to correct this or fix that. Jon was co-dependent and thus had his own problem with not being able to say no and not wanting to disappoint anyone. So he always jumped up and helped Lee.

At 6:00 p.m., Lee would stop for a brandy with Jon and talk until about 8:00. Whether Jon enjoyed this, we'll never know. One morning, after an evening brandy, Lee was at the peak of his perfection addiction, pushing and pushing on Jon. Jon was working to meet Lee's demands but nothing he did was enough. Thirty minutes after Lee left his office, Jon, 46 years old, died of a heart attack. Lee felt extremely remorseful at the funeral and for weeks and weeks after. Going to the funeral didn't resolve his guilt. At the Christmas party, he got out Jon's old brandy and gave a toast in his honor. In a trembling voice, he asked others to speak about Jon. They felt grief as well but they didn't have unexpressed apologies to make to Jon. Lee felt alone with his burden.

If Lee had been aware of the effect his perfectionism had on others, he could have apologized to Jon. As it was, after Jon's death Lee became very conscious of how his behavior affected his employees and, for the first time in his life, he began taking steps to heal.

## Step 10
### We continued to take personal inventory and when we were wrong promptly admitted it.

Step 10 keeps us from becoming pompous and restores our humility. It is a maintenance step that helps us continue to accept our humanness and limitations.

When many others in the corporation are also keeping up with their own personal inventory, it generates a healthy productive environment where people aren't defensive. They want to be the best they can be. The Professional Growth Plan, we will see later, demonstrates a system to keep personal inventory as an ongoing process.

## Step 11
### We are now safe to let our entrepreneurial spirit come back to life.

We have come full circle from a bound-up place where we could barely be productive to being able to tap into a renewed source of energy and creativity. By mastering Steps 1 through

11, we have earned the right to be our true selves. In this state we can lose ourselves in our work. As Durant described it, the meaning of life is found in getting so absorbed in one's work that when we are done, life is a little better than it was before.

Take a minute to visualize a time when you were happy and productive in your work. Feel the feeling you had then. Remember that it is always available, again and again.


### Step 12
**Having recaptured our entrepreneurial spirit,
we carried this message to others whom we saw
imprisoned in resistance to their own productiveness.**


Tony was a supervisor for a crisis-oriented organization. As a recovering alcoholic, Tony had mastered all 11 Steps and was ready for Step 12. He began by reading a book his boss recommended, Elyahu Goldratt's *The Goal, A Process of On-going Improvement.* Then he suggested that his co-workers read it as well. This was his comment: "For 21 years I just came to work and did what I was told to do on my job, never questioning it. After reading *The Goal,* I don't become defensive any more when someone asks a question. I also looked around and found far better ways to do things and to be better at my work. Now I want to go back to school and get more tools so we can reach the goal — to make money."

Sharing the job and the aliveness that productive work can bring to people is a true gift to others as well as to the giver. Of all the lectures and tapes on motivation, nothing is as productively inspiring as healing ourselves from within and rejuvenating our own natural, original entrepreneurial spirit.

# 6

# Healthy Corporate Planning

To heal sabotaging or addictive behavior at the corporate level means that you examine what you have been doing and think about what you should begin to do. This recognition of past counterproductive behavior and contemplation of future productive behavior is the essence of planning.

You might have been able to get by 20 years ago, putting a business plan together without any strategic planning — but not today. The very essence of growth is change and how would one know a change has succeeded without looking at both the past and the future?

Every major competitor is concerned with your productivity. Some of this competition is obvious and some is covert but all of it is interested in you. So let's assume we have decided to create a healthy corporate plan.

The availability of high technology could tempt us to overuse analytical models and quantifiable data. The enticement here is to use these methods in the absence of strategic planning and fool ourselves into thinking our planning pro-

This chapter has been written by Richard Noland, Ph.D., a management consultant from Salem, Oregon.

cess is complete. To avoid this pitfall, we will include high tech data to support our goals but not vice-versa.

The awareness of a need for "high touch," on the other hand, could encourage endless meetings and discussions in the absence of analytical data. The temptation here is to avoid analyzing the results of the planning process and to fool oneself into thinking that the planning is founded in reality.

The whole point of a healthy corporate planning session is to fully merge both worlds — to use quantifiable data and opinions/feelings. Strategic planning can be very useful in and of itself. Its whole point is to bring convergence among executives and board members about why the company exists and where it should be heading, to create honest values, missions and goals.

## Conducting A Strategic Planning Session

There appear to be as many ways to run a strategic planning session as there are consultants willing to oversee and chair them. This should be looked at as an asset, however — not a weakness. In strategic planning, it is the process that is important, not the product. Don't waste time trying to find the perfect format or agenda. Instead, actively seek out different facilitators with different formats. Most formats include concepts like mission statements, objectives, strategies, goals and strengths/weaknesses. Most planning sessions involve both the board of directors and the management team.

Every group or person who has veto power over your business activities and who has made use of that power must be included in the strategic planning session. Be sure to get those vocal leaders and opinion-makers involved. Resist the temptation to leave out a troublemaker. The whole point of the strategic planning session is to bring out different points of view so they can be addressed and moved to a convergence of vision. Even if participants exercise addictive or sabotaging behavior styles, it is still more important to have those participants present than to have a smoother running planning session. The facilitator can adjust to controlling the impact of counterproductive behavior patterns.

The most successful planning sessions are those in which there is a lot of disagreement and controversy. It is the discussion, along with the give and take of forthright people, that helps assure us that the interest and the views of the customers will be voiced. Look at the differing opinions as a resource, not a threat, and don't be afraid to invite comment.

Next, the facilitator — always be sure the facilitator is someone who takes charge of the planning session. It is critical that no board member, manager or CEO run the meetings or dominate them. This can be prevented only by choosing a trained, assertive facilitator who will control the session without being obtrusive. Running a strategic planning session without an outside facilitator is rarely successful for several reasons. First, regardless of an insider's attempt to act objectively, there is always the danger that he or she will be perceived as running his or her own agenda or bowing to an aggressive opinion-maker in the group. Second, if this person is good, you need him or her as a participant, not an objective bystander. Third, an insider's experience as a facilitator is often more limited than a professional's, so the process developed for the meeting may reflect too narrow a view of strategic planning.

During strategic planning sessions, time should always be dedicated to focusing on the past, the present and the future. Some facilitators spend too little time on the past, believing that strategy is being formed for the future. In a way that is correct but they're also making the assumption that everyone knows why your business exists and what it's all about.

To plan where you want to go, it's necessary to know where you are now. That's why every strategic planning session must include data on the present. If someone says it's too boring or they don't understand the current report, then they must be educated or else their ignorance will be a millstone around the necks of the rest of the planners. If you don't understand the current position, you have no business voicing opinions about the future.

The future is often the fun part of strategic planning. More opinions will be given during this part of the planning process than at any other time. That's fine; that's the way it should be. All efforts should be made to encourage even the most reticent participant to share his or her vision of the future. Since the degree of consensus about the future is directly correlated to the degree of consensus about the past and present, if you want to make this stage easier, spend more time on the first two stages.

To allow enough time for the strategic planning session, plan a weekend away from home where nothing can interrupt the process. At the very least, the session should be an all day affair, with a commitment from all parties involved to stay with it from beginning to end. It is deadly to the planning process to let anyone, even a key individual, come late or leave early. People arriving late will dampen the enthusiasm and mood of the session.

The steps outlined below are an example of a planning session. We call this format "Exploiting the Inevitable." It is designed to get the board and management team moving in the same direction by emphasizing that external pressures will inevitably affect their business, whether they like it or not. Productivity is often a goal which relies as much on external variables as it does on internal variables.

Break the group up into four smaller groups, maintaining a mix of the management team and board members. You may wish to designate each team, for example, one team as Finance, one as Operations, one as Marketing, and one as Human Resources. Periodically during the session, the four teams will form to brainstorm issues and then report back to the larger group.

## Past

To exploit the inevitable, it's necessary to understand the company's past and all the factors that will affect its future. The first step focuses on creating a common understanding of the company's history and what should be factored into any future plans. Three subparts of this phase are: examination of the company's "stakeholders," its strengths and its weaknesses. A stakeholder is defined as any individual, group or organization that can be affected by or have an impact on your company. This includes such entities as financial institutions, regulators, customers, etc.

The first brainstorming session, meant to identify stakeholders, has three stages. To start, each team has five minutes to devise a list of generic groups of stakeholders (called Level One Stakeholders) such as government, financial institutions and local businesses. The teams then reconvene and share their lists, blending the four lists into one master list.

Again, divide the teams into the original four, supplying each with copies of the master list (either all of it or a quarter of it), from which they are to develop a list of Level Two Stakeholders, specific entities within the groups identified in Level One. Once again, the four teams come together to share lists. When everyone understands and identifies the various entities, each member prioritizes the list.

Next, everyone lists the entities and rates them on a scale of 1 (Not Important) to 5 (Very Important). You may be surprised at the number of stakeholders identified. Planning participants are often surprised as well. One board member remarked after this exercise that he had a whole new appreciation for the CEO because of the 133 identified stakeholders that the CEO must deal with.

Having identified stakeholders and their relative importance to the company, the focus now turns to strengths and weaknesses. This is done in two stages, first focusing on strengths and then on weaknesses. Follow the same routine used for stakeholders, dividing into teams, then reporting back to develop a comprehensive list of their findings. Allocate time for explaining items on the lists, when necessary, but limit the explanations so there are no long, drawn-out dissertations. You'll find that putting the strengths and weaknesses on a flip chart goes a long way toward tuning everyone's thoughts.

Brainstorming about the company's stakeholders, strengths and weaknesses will articulate the past of the company in a surprisingly efficient and noncontroversial way.

## Present

The next part of the strategic planning session is the present. Oddly enough, the first step here is to envision the future. What you do in the present is influenced by where you think you will be in the future. The visioning exercise consists of two steps.

The first step is to envision the company's environment in five years. This is where discussions about political and economic trends at local, state and national levels take place.

The second phase of the visioning exercise is to discuss where in that environment the company will be in five years. It is useful to discuss several visions at this point. For example, two of the groups could contemplate a worst-case scenario while the other two could present a best-case scenario. The important thing is that there be a good discussion about where the corporation will be in five years. This exercise should end with a comprehensive view of what the group wants the corporation to look like five years from now.

At this point, group participants have considered stakeholders, strengths, weaknesses and a vision of the environment and the company's place in it. Out of all this discussion will come concerns about the company and where it is headed. Have the group list those concerns which come from their area of concentration.

This part of the planning process should produce all the individual concerns on which people take stands. If handled correctly, the rest of the session will be a piece of cake! Everyone will have had an opportunity to get his or her issue on the table.

## Future

The next stage of the strategic planning process is to examine what the company **should** be about. Some strategic planners call this step the mission statement. Much time is spent to come up with one or two unspecific sentences conveying some lofty, idealistic and moral goal. We prefer to call that a philosophy and reserve the name of mission statement for a more dynamic role in the strategic planning process. Therefore, we call this stage a Statement of Philosophy and look at it during a brief discussion. Don't spend a lot of time looking for nonoffensive words (e.g. *service* instead of *profits*) or making sure the phrasing is all-encompassing. The point of this exercise is to have a discussion of the philosophy of your business and how it is revealed in day-to-day activities.

After this, we turn our attention to the immediate. Each team is charged with preparing two mission action statements for the coming year. We are not concerned about how precise the wording is, simply that each group should have two mission action statements to guide the work in their area for the next year. An example of a mission action statement for the Finance group might be, "**Have a financially sound business.**" Mission action statements are to be seen as dynamic and responding to the issues facing the company in the coming year. Their broad, generic nature, however, necessitates that they be finely tuned into strategies. The next phase of the strategic planning session, therefore, is to reduce the mission action statements to strategies with clearly defined due dates and persons responsible for accomplishment.

At this point, the immediate future should be addressed. The stakeholders, the strengths and weaknesses, the visions of the future, the concerns of the group regarding the company and, finally, the philosophy which underlies the business's activities are the data bank from which mission statements come and out of which objectives, goals and strategies are formed. Everyone should now be ready to work on the strategy for the coming year's operation.

Since the teams have each identified two mission action statements for their respective areas, the next step is to develop objectives for these mission action statements. The individual teams do this by brainstorming all the roadblocks to accomplishing it. For example, the financial mission action statement — **Have a financially sound business** — may encounter some roadblocks, such as cost overruns on employee wages and benefits. It is important that the group stay with the brain-

storming and develop a comprehensive list of all the things
that could be roadblocks to the mission action statement.

## Developing Solutions

Once this list is made, you will look at those roadblocks as
opportunities. The group now turns its attention to developing
solutions. The first step here is to list each roadblock and
discuss solutions. For example, the roadblock of cost overruns
might be solved by accurate weekly reports of employee
costs, perhaps development of a functional cost analysis for
each position and cost justification for each proposed new
position. These solutions, once identified, are listed as objectives. Then you may want to prioritize the objectives, particularly if there are a lot of them.

The next step is to discuss each objective and list specific
goals for the objective which are quantified, when possible,
have a target date for completion and a specific person responsible for implementation. For example, the objective of
developing a functional cost analysis of each position could
result in a goal like, "**The Accounting Department will research and propose a functional cost analysis program to
the CEO by March 1. The person in charge of this goal will
be the head accountant.**" It is not necessary that the goals be
articulated in such detail as to specify the way they are to be
accomplished. That is the purpose of the strategy, the last part
of strategic planning.

It is good management practice not to pursue strategies in
the strategic planning meeting. The company has hired
talented managers and a CEO to accomplish goals within
their areas of responsibility. In fact, it is sometimes recommended that the strategic planning session end with the
mission action statements, allowing the management team to
continue developing objectives, goals and strategies. The
board's time restraints and expertise should influence the
degree of board involvement in objectives and goals but the
implementation should definitely be left to the respective

managers. Their strategies, however, should be reported back to the CEO.

Each goal, then, should have a strategy, a way to accomplish it. An example of part of the strategy for the goal "**The Accounting Department will research and propose a functional cost analysis program to the CEO by March 1**" would be: "**Sue will contact software vendors and compile a list of appropriate computer programs by January 15.**" The strategies become a recipe for the accomplishment of the goal. They should be detailed enough so that if anyone in the department followed the strategy, the goal would, in fact, be accomplished.

There are some things to be careful of when developing strategies. After writing the strategy, make sure you can answer the question, "How do I know if I've achieved it?" For example, you may have a strategy stating that "**There will be effective control of overtime.**" How do you know when you have accomplished this? Does effective control of overtime mean no overtime, half of last year's overtime, the same level as last year — or what? Who is to control this — and how? A better strategy statement is: "**Supervisors will be charged with monitoring overtime and reporting it to the Operations officer on a weekly basis so that steps can be taken to keep overtime below last year's level by hiring a part-time employee.**" When we discuss the Professional Growth Plan we will describe a system to articulate strategy and goals.

Sometimes strategies are criticized as being too much work in writing the obvious. One reason for this is the lack of precise wording in what is to be accomplished and when. Words like "ongoing," "adequate" and "effective" are too vague for strategic planning statements. For example, it's obvious that employees should have an ongoing attitude of pleasantness that adequately reflects hospitality to customers in such a way that effective service is rendered. This statement, however, is not very useful to strategic planning. On the other hand, consider a statement telling the reader: "**A seminar on customer relations will be conducted at the beginning of each quarter. Employees will attend the seminar to improve** service." This statement is more informative and useful. It is a strategy while the former is more like an objective.

Every strategy should be related to a goal, which is related to an objective, which is related to a mission action statement. It is advisable to code or letter the strategies so they can always be defended, partly on the merit of the mission action statements developed at the planning session.

This process of developing strategy has finally brought us into the realm of the business plan, where the strategies become an important element of the plan. However, before you move on to the business plan, remember that in strategic planning, it is the process that's critical. Everything that's produced in a strategic planning session should be viewed as dynamic but subject to change. In fact, the process is so critical and dynamic in today's changing environment that some businesses are having strategic planning sessions every six months. It is advisable that different facilitators and formats be used from time to time so that issues can be approached from different directions and so that the emphasis of the planning is allowed to change with the needs of the company.

The Professional Growth Plan which we will discuss will help you in the planning process by showing you a system that can assist you to articulate goals and transform them into strategies. It will also help by providing a high touch system that will assist you in communicating those strategies to every individual within the corporation.

# 7

# Implementing The Corporate Plan

Creating a healthy corporate plan is a major accomplishment. The key is to make sure this gold nugget is assimilated into the corporation in such a way that employees will honor it, safeguard it and make it happen! The Professional Growth Plan which we will discuss here has been successful in keeping corporate plans alive and progressing.

Many companies have spent time and money on retreats or sessions to design a corporate plan. When they attempt to assimilate the plan into the rest of the company, it is met with blank stares, token nods, unbacked promises and/or indignant protests. Without planning for the assimilation, the new plan rarely makes it to implementation. One major reason for this is the unhealthy, unproductive systems we have discussed throughout this book, the most common of which is the traditional performance review process.

## Eliminating Nonproductive Performance Reviews

Let's first examine the most frequently used performance
review systems. Our research indicates that there are currently
three prevalent employee review systems. Each has a basic
flaw that severely limits its usefulness to a healthy corporation.

Type A performance reviews are unstructured. The reviewer/
supervisor simply describes the employee's strengths and
weaknesses by writing at least one long, analytical paragraph
about the employee.

Type B performance reviews are more structured. Management gives the reviewer a scale on which to rate an employee's
performance from Excellent to Unfavorable. Scores are recorded
for such factors as communication, promptness, quantity of
work, ability to delegate tasks and adherence to dress code.

Type C performance reviews incorporate a major new component added during the 1970s and 1980s — "mutual goal
setting." This hybrid simply adds goal setting to an existing A or
B type review. The type C review is presented as a productivity
tool. The employee is often asked to write his own job goals.

Do the A, B and C review systems actually affect an employee's productiveness? Or do the flaws of review systems
block their effectiveness?

## Type A Performance Review

With a type A performance review, it is assumed the supervisor is a competent writer, both comfortable with the idea
and well-equipped to compose a series of grammatically
correct paragraphs. There is no doubt that many supervisors
are able to generate high performance from their employees,
yet have never developed good writing skills. Consequently,
the review process is either assigned to a personnel manager
or not done at all. In both cases there will be a lack of direct
feedback from the supervisor to the employee on either the
strategic plan or a daily task.

Type A reviews also depend upon a second assumption.
They assume that a supervisor is competent to both analyze

and correctly describe how effectively an employee is performing. At a 1980 seminar, most supervisors for a group of nuclear physicists confessed they avoided giving performance reviews — most had never given one. The company's general manager stated the reason. Each physicist considered his job too specialized to be either adequately analyzed or competently described by another.

But let's assume supervisors have completed well-written statements that describe an employee's effectiveness. Are the reports effective in increasing productivity? Rarely. In fact, the reports are frequently counterproductive.

Reviewers have generally gathered and collated information from only one point of view — their own. In fact, employees may never even have been consulted. Also, reviewers assume the position of judges. Consequently the report becomes more an indictment than a review. The indictment is more likely to be because the supervisor does not like the employee than because the employee is not meeting profit goals.

In the late 1970s, many divisions of a Fortune 500 Corporation were using type A performance reviews. One division hired a research team of five PhDs for a research project. Because no one on the research team wanted to be team manager, the division president hired a 24-year-old recent MBA graduate, Marge, to manage the team.

Two of the team members, Sam and Roger, became father figures for Marge. Both men had worked with young people and had daughters about Marge's age. Two other team members, Mary and Ruth, were in their mid-thirties. Both had attended college during the 1960s and graduated with counter-culture ideas. Despite the differences in their backgrounds and appearances, Marge, Mary and Ruth got along well.

The last team member, Judy, was also in her mid-thirties. Her role in the project differed significantly from the others'. Judy's assignment, to arrange for product testing with customers and carry feedback from the field back to the team, kept her out of the office most of the time. Judy attended fewer staff meetings and followed fewer office guidelines than the other team members. Marge seemed to resent having so little control over Judy's work and schedule. The tension between the two surfaced when Judy received a letter of commendation from a customer. Marge accused Judy of soliciting the praise. She did not accept Judy's explanation that the compliments were spontaneously given by a satisfied customer.

At the end of the year, the president asked Marge for a type A performance review on each member of the team. A competent writer, she nevertheless felt awkward judging seven people who surpassed her in age, experience and knowledge of their work. But her addiction to control eased the way.

Sam and Roger were the easiest to review. These father figures were applauded for their support, their loyalty and their understanding. Mary and Ruth received reviews that commended them on their good communication skills, their adherence to rules and their promptness at meetings. Shortly after these reviews were distributed, Marge was laid off.

Judy's review was not given to her directly and had been secretly forwarded to the president's office instead. The review was very critical and accused Judy of lack of integrity with clients. Marge cited soliciting commendations as an example. No illustration supported the second accusation — Judy's alleged lack of commitment to the company. The review concluded with the statement that Judy needed much improvement.

Do we know anything more of the progress of this project because of these performance reviews? Very little! We do, however, know more about the relationships Marge established with the team. We know that Marge liked Sam and Roger. But do their reviews show how each man contributed to the research goal of the company? Marge's relationship with Ruth and Mary was also successful. But are we getting any new data about their contribution to the research goal of the company?

Marge and Judy disliked each other. How did this affect the project? Did Judy refuse to perform some important tasks for the team? Judy's letter of commendation from a customer seems to indicate that from one very important point of view, she was doing a superior job. Yet her performance review was derogatory. As you can see from the Marge/Judy scenario, type A performance reviews are likely to be unproductive management tools. In our example, Marge with undergraduate work in English and an advanced degree in Business, overcame the first barrier. She had well-trained and competent writing skills. Her ability to put together a grammatically correct paragraph regarding each member of the team was unquestionable. Marge's addictive patterns, however, were not sufficient to overcome the second barrier in type A assessments. She was not forthright enough to analyze effective performance as it relates to a corporate plan. Instead she substituted a description of her positive or negative emotional involvement with each member of the team. A third problem also surfaced. Instead of reaffirming the team's commitment to their common task and reinforcing each individual's self-esteem, Marge severely undermined at least one individual. The manner in which she handled Judy's review did nothing to further the team's work. It did cause sabotage.

## Type B Performance Review

Type B performance reviews attempt to rectify some of type A's problems. The usual type B performance review preselects certain areas to evaluate. Communication, promptness, quality and quantity of work, ability to delegate, dress and technical knowledge are common areas often included. Next, a rating scale is established. An employee can score between Excellent and Unsatisfactory in each skill area. Or, if the system is numerical, between 1 and 5.

This system obviously eliminates one major disadvantage of type A reviews — the need for a paragraph of good grammatical writing. Instead, it codifies a manager's observation into a supposedly more objective evaluation tool that focuses the manager on the performance of the employee, not his or her own writing skills.

But, we have already seen in the Marge/Judy example how dangerous it is to assume that a manager is truly objective. Do the predetermined categories and rating scales really create a more objective system of review?

It is the rare manager (4%) who does not have his or her own addictive or co-dependent patterns, cancelling the ability to be an impartial judge. Most managers have a difficult time appreciating their opposites.

Whenever an employee is confronted with low scores, there is a desire to numb the discomfort. This can be done by disputing the evaluator's opinions. The illusion of objectivity, however, makes it much harder for an employee to understand that a score of Unsatisfactory could be one person's disguised feeling about his reaction to the employee. Similarly, a score of Excellent could be the manager's fear of hurting the employee's feelings. Both lead to an unproductive activity which is not conducive to the realization of corporate goals.

Type B performance reviews, then, still retain a major flaw. They set a judgmental relationship between supervisor and employee which reflects the worst aspects of addictiveness and co-dependency.

Linda, a former high school teacher who also had experience in public relations, was hired by a major U.S. city as a junior personnel analyst. Her first assignment was to tackle a problem the department had avoided for three years. The city's Police Department had a large number of vacant clerk/typist positions. Potential applicants hesitated to apply since the job had a reputation for slow promotability. The goal, as outlined to Linda by her supervisor, was to entice sufficient numbers of clerk/typists to fill the vacant jobs.

Linda, a creative and energetic person, interviewed and photographed happy, high-level, successful Police Department clerk/typists, then arranged the material into an attractive brochure. The project took 60 days from start to finish and was entirely successful. The brochure helped fill all the vacant clerk/typist positions within three weeks.

Soon after, Linda met with her supervisor for a type B review. Under Professional Behavior, Linda's supervisor had checked needs improvement. Not wanting to lose the job, Linda asked her boss to be more specific about her professional behavior.

"How, specifically, can I improve?" she asked. He replied, "You walk too fast, laugh too much. And you do not take the job seriously enough."

Pursuing the point Linda said, "So . . . what you want from me is to walk slower, subdue my laughter and act more serious about the job?"

The supervisor, who had done such reviews for 11 years, was stunned and angry. Apparently no one had ever questioned his judgment or addiction to routine. He quickly changed the subject and ended the session.

This performance review did more potential harm than good. It embarrassed the supervisor by putting him in a position of defining a category on the "report card" — professionalism. It alienated Linda by ignoring her creative and timely contribution. In fact, the review created an unbridgeable chasm between two co-workers. More tragically, it gave two people, both interested in contributing positively to their work commitment, no way to deal with the future.

## Type C Performance Review

Type C performance review attempts to do just that — deal with the future.

During the 1980s, management recognized that if reviews were going to contribute to productivity, they should not only evaluate the past performance of an employee but it was equally important they should find ways to foster high levels of future performance. Type C performance reviews added a new component, goal setting, to existing performance review models. The new style review became type A plus goal setting or type B plus goal setting. (See Appendix 6.)

The American Management Association courses began to emphasize goal setting. McGraw-Hill published a film on performance review which included this new point of view. Interpersonal Management Skills courses sponsored by Learning International Systems stressed not only the addition of goals for an employee but also ways to measure the achievement of these goals. Many large management consulting firms were developing and marketing a type C review.

In each course, there was one constantly repeated theme: It is extremely important for managers and employees to set goals **together**.

One intellectual leader of this goal setting movement was Peter E. Drucker. He saw a need for managers to answer the famous question, "What business are we in?" — selling widgets, one billion Band-Aids, customer service, quality, etc. There was such hunger for this type of clarity and objectivity in management that large and small companies throughout the United States adopted Drucker's "Management by Objectives" (MBO) as their basic management tool. Performance reviews with specific objectives remained the dominant style in the '70s and '80s.

Unfortunately, the system did not produce the results expected. Not only did many employees show great resistance to adopting management's objectives as their own, in some cases they actually avoided doing work which would produce the desired results. Managers and employees alike became discouraged about a review system that took so much time and produced such modest results and the forms, books and seminars went unused.

A major leasing company adopted the management-by-objective approach in 1973. They called their program "Target Performance Planning" or TPP. The leasing company hired a consultant to help plan and implement the program. The consultant talked first with the president of the company, then with the vice-president of each profit center and so on down through layers of management, ending with second-level supervisors. First-level supervisors and employees were never interviewed.

The company proudly published its chosen objectives in a 20-page brochure. Elaborate charts illustrated the text. Pages of copy described goals and objectives and how to implement the system. Only one line of copy reminded managers to "get employee input, so that the goal is mutual." The summary of objectives was both terse and simple. It came down to four words: more, better, bigger, faster.

All performance was measured, of course, against these objectives. Second-level supervisors met with the vice-presidents of profit centers for reviews. Most often, performance fell short. In the discussion that followed, supervisors gave reasons, usually good ones, for not reaching their goals. The last phase of each interview included stating new goals and arranging new time frames.

Even though supervisors who missed objectives also missed important monetary rewards, compliance with the MBOs didn't improve. The lure of additional money did not seem to affect the quality or timeliness of a supervisor's achievement. As discussed earlier, money has been found to rank seventh in importance as a motivator. But this leasing company, like many others, did not believe it.

Top management assumed that each profit center director was committed to the company's goals and objectives. Yet, typically, top management did not know how to get commitment from the employees who would implement them. This is not meant to be an indictment of either corporate management or key senior managers. Indeed, they were sharp, professional, committed managers who were well-educated, experienced and competent. Rather, we use this example to point out an important flaw in type C performance reviews based on Management by Objectives. Unless the company first "touches" managers (i.e., finds out what they need and then commits to their nonmaterial requests — high touch — in exchange for their commitment to the company's goals), Management by Objectives will fail.

We can see that Management by Objectives often becomes goal setting from the top down. One level of management presents its objectives to the managers below them. The system creates subtle resistance, lack of cooperation, disinterest and passivity. It lacks high touch.

When a goal is handed down to employees from management, they may be intimidated into accepting the goal without any input. The result is a lack of commitment to meet it. Only through the effort to define what employees need to carry out a specific objective can they develop a real commitment.

The ideal of managers and employees setting goals mutually is rarely achieved. First, the strategic/business planning session can rarely include all the employees. It would be mass chaos. And we have observed that employees do not always want to be in on the strategic planning. Many employees are asking for the goals — they just want to know what they are. Changing the goals is not a major motivator to employees, so why mess with the gold nugget plan from the planning session? True mutual goal setting is done in an entirely different manner as we will see later on.

Given that there are so many problems with performance reviews, should we eliminate them altogether? If, in fact, they are not contributing to corporate productivity goals, should they go the way of the slide rule? We don't think so. Control of our organizations demands systematic feedback and track records of employee performance. But we do need to create a new system of performance review that eliminates the flaws. We need a performance review system that overcomes the problems of types A, B and C.

Let's imagine a performance review system that does not require the reviewer to be a good writer, that does not put the reviewer into a position of addictive reaction, that does not deliver an empty set of goals to the employee to work through, that does touch employees and does increase profitability. Does this sound possible? It not only is possible but it has, in fact, been tested in 25 companies all over the country since 1981.

In 1979 a group of researchers and trainers at a division of Xerox developed a multi-million dollar performance system that became known as the Professional Growth Plan. This Professional Growth Plan incorporates all the benefits of types A, B and C review systems without their inherent flaws. In fact, the uniqueness of this performance review system is that it increases morale and productivity at the same time.

## Initiating The Professional Growth Plan

The Professional Growth Plan treats every employee as a **professional** in his or her work; **growth** is about the future, about doing more, better, faster; **plan** is its part in the strategic business plan. The review system should include these basic objectives: (1) to improve productivity, (2) to implement the strategic and business plan, (3) to increase employee job satisfaction and (4) to decrease addictive/nonproductive activities.

The Professional Growth Plan incorporates these concepts in the following four simple steps.

## Step 1

Skills most important to the employee's job are discussed. A Pre-Review form (Appendix 5, Step I) listing various job skills, is completed by both employee and reviewer before the review meeting. At the meeting, both discuss the relative importance of each skill to the job. The employee is not discussed at this point. (See instructions, Appendix 4.)

It is not crucial that the employee and reviewer agree on these points. It is crucial that each sees how the other views the job. Very often, low morale develops when an employee spends all his energy on skill $x$. Then, at promotion time, an employee performing skill $y$ gets the promotion. The first employee might gladly have developed $y$ but his supervisor did not tell him it was most important.

With the Professional Growth Plan, when both the supervisor and employee rate priorities and define important job activities, everyone benefits in the end.

## Step 2

Discuss the job tasks that the employee performs well (Appendix 5, Step II). In this step, the pre-review form offers the same list of job-related skills as in step 1. Again, before the meeting, both parties have checked areas where each feels the employee is strong. In the Professional Growth Plan there is no discussion of the employee's weakness.

You may think it's Pollyannaish to tell people their strengths but not their weaknesses, that it's unrealistic. Remember, our aim is to increase productivity, not to judge and criticize. Dale Carnegie would often say, "No one was ever changed through criticism." We usually criticize based on what behaviors in others expose our own addictive/obsessive patterns. Thus it is of little or no value.

Xerox Learning Systems once surveyed different types of employees. These employees were asked what motivated them to do a good job. The overwhelming majority said,

"Recognition." If recognition is built firmly into the review, it will occur. Recognition is the main function of step 2.

Further, the employee's weaknesses are handled in step 3, goal setting. They are dealt with by stating what we want from the employee in order to meet the profit goal, not what they do that irritates us.

### Step 3

Set mutual goals. This is the heart of the Professional Growth Plan (Appendix 4). During the Professional Growth Plan meeting, the supervisor and employee perform essentially similar roles. Specifically, each comes to the review meeting prepared to tell the other what he or she could do to make the job more likely to meet the corporate goals.

When asked point blank or given a piece of paper to fill in, an employee might say he wants "more communication." But in preparing for the PGP meeting, using the funnel questioning process (see Appendix 7), the employee request becomes:

> **The number one thing I need from my supervisor to make me more productive is:** to meet with me every Wednesday, 11:00-11:15, to give me feedback on certain tasks I perform, particularly scheduling, cost estimates and inventory. **How achieved?** Let me know how I am doing on scheduling, let me know how close I am on cost estimates and let me know if I am saving any money with our new inventory control process. **What would be different?** I would be well under budget and missed deadlines would decrease 25%. (See Appendix 8, Most Common Employee Requests.)

In a separate office the reviewer also prepared steps 1, 2 and 3 in advance. One reviewer request was:

> **The number one thing I want from you that will help us reach our profit goal is:** write up a daily schedule and plan every afternoon for the next day. **How achieved?** Include the priorities for the day, who works which machine, estimated time on each machine and

allow for some down time. **What would be different?**
We'd get production started at 7:00 a.m. each day in-
stead of 8:00 a.m. (See Appendix 9, Most Common
Reviewer Requests.)

## Step 4

Alignment between the employee's responsibility for the
strategic plan and the employee's specific request is very
different from the mutual goal setting concept of the 1980s.
Mutual goal setting was used to get employee to buy-in on
corporate goals, i.e., to have employees help establish their
own work goals. While for some employees the corporate
goal may indeed be top priority, 95% of employee requests
come from their own personal needs (recognition, challenge,
security, etc.). These needs are the employees' truths about
what they need in order to be genuinely interested and focused on company goals. The lie is to pretend that every
employee cares about profit and productivity. The truth is that
if employees get their needs met, they are much more conscious of and committed to their supervisors' goals.

Our research has shown that most employees prefer to
have managers and CEOs establish corporate goals. They are
the ones who see the market, the economy and the competition; the employee usually welcomes a strategic plan, especially one that comes from a healthy planning session.

In mutual goal setting of the '80s, the strategic plan was so
changed by the time everyone put in their two cents, there
remained hardly any resemblance to the original goal which
may have been, for example, 10% net profit after taxes. The
CEO and the executives have a legitimate right and obligation
to set the goal. The productive and effective place for employees and supervisors to have input is to tell what they
need in order to accomplish their part of the already set
strategic plan.

The Professional Growth Plan in step 4 aligns manager and
employee together vis-à-vis their goals. Step 4 is documented

on a colored sheet to represent that this is a combination of
what both parties want in order to achieve the profit goals
(Appendices 10 and 11).

The employee always goes first; therefore, item 1 represents
an employee request. If the supervisor agrees, they write it on
the colored sheet. Employee items (Appendix 8) are most
likely to be quite different from employer requests and can
usually be categorized as respect, recognition or freedom,
although those three words are rarely used. In our research
and consulting since 1979, we have gone over thousands of
employee requests. Ninety-five percent of the time, employees ask for recognition, respect or freedom in their own
terms, in exchange for carrying out the corporate goal.

By being asked to make an individual request on his own
and by having it heard, written and followed through by his
supervisor, the employee is touched in the way designed by
the high tech/high touch dynamic.

Item 2 on the colored PGP Results Sheet is the supervisor's
request. Supervisors' requests almost always call for more,
better or faster. They are very different from employee requests.
Thus, the Alignment (colored) sheet is lining up what the
employee wants next to what the supervisor wants from him.
It is an illusion to pretend that employee and reviewer would
have a truly mutual goal. In Management by Objectives, the
Supervisor's request is agreed to by the employee and that is
called mutual. This does not touch the employee. Items indi-
cating an employee was touched are sampled in Appendix 8.

So, Alignment in the Professional Growth Plan combines,
lines up, the separate and unique requests of employee
(Goal 1), then supervisor (Goal 2), then employee (Goal 3),
then supervisor (Goal 4). Supervisors' requests relate to their
responsibility to meet the corporate goal. Employees' requests
let management know their individual motivation. No more
does management have to figure out how to motivate employees — **the employees will tell you themselves** — but
only if they have the opportunity to be guided through the
funnel process to very clearly and thoroughly let the supervisor know exactly how to fulfill their requests so that employees truly feel touched, i.e., acknowledged.

## Summary

In summary, the Professional Growth Plan begins with a healthy corporate plan. The CEO and executive staff each separately follow the four steps of the PGP to align their requests and company goals. Then it is used by every manager, supervisor and employee in the organization.

The PGP is a nonaddictive, productive two-way communication process which is used to take the results of the strategic planning session and tie it to each individual in the company. Simultaneous to spreading the profit goals, it fulfills employee's need to be touched (acknowledged, included, heard).

The Professional Growth Plan, which can replace and eliminate unproductive performance reviews, provides the following.

(1) It ties employee activities to the profit goals.
(2) It opens the minds of both parties for a brief time.
(3) It shifts frustrations into productive requests, stated in positive terms only.
(4) It sets out what each needs from the other to be more productive.
(5) It draws out the true high touch item of each employee.
(6) It aligns two promises and two requests for each boss/employee agreement.
(7) It creates productive conversation and activities as a way of life.
(8) It eliminates many opportunities for addictive and co-dependent behaviors.
(9) It follows up the aligned goals every 90 days.
(10) It documents those who kept their agreements.
(11) It provides a monthly corporate culture report.

Items 9, 10 and 11, the follow-up, is such a powerful and unique breakthrough for the healthy corporation of the 1990s that it requires an entire chapter. Next we will focus on keeping the corporate plan alive by following up on all the smaller goals agreed to in the Professional Growth Plan.

8

# The Follow-Up System

## What Is It?

The purpose of the follow-up system is to assure that corporate profit goals are met or exceeded. It is a tracking process to monitor the commitments that were established to reach these profit goals.

Bringing integrity to the commitments and agreements reached between supervisors and employees is a key part of the follow-up system. Recognizing that the PGP commitments are directly related to corporate profit and specifically designed to touch employees, a carefully monitored step-by-step follow-up system combining regimentation, professionalism and sensitivity is critical.

## Who Is In Charge?

Computer Aided Drafting and Design (CADD) operators did not exist 20 years ago because the technology was not yet developed. The same is true of a person responsible for

corporate health. The introduction of the 12-Step program
into the workplace is a revolutionary new concept. The Professional Growth Plan is transformational to employer/em-
ployee communication. To meet these new challenges of
corporate healing, we believe a new position should be
created for the person in charge of monitoring the follow-up
process. We shall refer to this person as the "Vice-President
for Corporate Vision" (VPCV).

During the past 30 years, the corporation and the individual
have become, to some extent, opposing forces. Synthesis, the
alignment and merging of two opposite forces, can renew the
partnership and go a step further toward creating a healthy
one. On the larger scale, the VPCV is charged with keeping the
corporate vision. On a day-to-day basis, he is charged with
merging the corporate goals with employees' touch needs.
They will lead the company through strategic planning sessions, the Professional Growth Plan and the follow-up. It is
recommended that the VPCV be an outside consultant contracted on a one-year basis. This would ensure that this
individual will not be involved in any current addictive/co-
dependent activities in the corporation. A constant concern of
the VPCV is the quality and timeliness of the monthly managers' reports as part of the follow-up system. It should be
agreed that the consulting contract will be terminated if the
managers' reports and 90-day feedback from both employees
and reviewers are not handled in a responsible and timely
manner. A sample job description for the VPCV is shown in
Appendix 15.

## How Can This Be Accomplished?

The flow chart shown in Appendix 12 outlines the follow-
up system. Appendices 10 and 11 displays the sheets referred
to at the beginning of the PGP follow-up system flow chart.
The follow-up process begins when the completed, signed
and dated Alignment sheets are given to the VPCV.

Upon receipt of the completed, signed and dated Alignment
sheets, the VPCV will enter the data into a computer to obtain

the information shown in Appendix 13. The next review should then be scheduled for 90 days after the first date recorded on the primary manager's report (as shown in Appendix 13). After 90 days, the sheet in Appendix 16 is given to the reviewer and the employee. If they are not filled in and returned within 48 hours, the VPCV should meet separately with each individual to assist in this process.

Asking people to be accountable for their commitments can be a very confrontational experience. It takes courage and self-confidence to pursue this point in the face of resistance, hostility or denial. Thus, the importance of selecting a competent, unbiased professional VPCV cannot be overemphasized.

## Case In Point

Dawn was the highest paid paraprofessional troubleshooter in an engineering firm. She harbored hidden feelings of inadequacy because, although extremely competent, she possessed neither an engineer's license nor even a college degree. To overcome these feelings, she longed for recognition and acknowledgement from her boss, Glen.

In preparing the Professional Growth Plan, Glen complained that he lost billable hours listening to Dawn explain, complain and give lengthy dialogues of her problem clients and difficult investigations in the field. In the funnel process (Appendix 7) he changed this complaint to a request. Instead of asking the same questions repeatedly, would Dawn keep a record of his answers, then work more independently to solve some of the problems on her own? When asked, "What would be different?" he replied, "I'd be able to bill 30 hours per week instead of 25."

When it was Dawn's turn, she was not totally honest in her request. This is understandable because her real issue was wanting recognition to overcome her hidden feelings of inadequacy — which is embarrassing to ask for. So instead she asked for "varied clients." Glen, believing this was the way Dawn wanted to be touched, granted her request for a more varied client base.

During the 90-day follow-up meeting, Dawn was asked if she followed through on Glen's request that she begin to solve her own problems in the field. She belittled the PGP, changed the subject, and said she was too busy for this game. We worked with Dawn through the funnel process once again and she was finally able to admit that she had not, in fact, kept her agreement with Glen (0%). Instead, she had continued to run into Glen's office and complain and explain, as before.

The pinch of admitting that we have not kept our word can open a stuck mind to new levels of understanding. In this case, new understanding led to a renewed request from Dawn that was more honest. She discovered her own need to be recognized for her expertise as a troubleshooter, particularly as the only nondegreed, nonlicensed engineer. She asked to have her role as a troubleshooter announced at a staff meeting, to be introduced to the clients as such and to be allowed to train a new paraprofessional, thus giving her the recognition and esteem she sought.

At last the real touch issue was recognized and Glen no longer had to listen to long narratives which were Dawn's subversive way of demanding recognition. Both parties were now winners and the company benefited with five more billable hours per week from Glen, and seven more billable hours per week from Dawn.

Thus we can see that when the VPCV meets individually to complete follow-up sheets, it isn't always a one minute stop. When these are not turned in, there is usually some reason for the delay. Most often, it is resistance on the part of the employee/reviewer.

When the follow-up sheets are collected, they add to the manager's monthly report. It becomes a manager's secondary report — secondary, because now we have a yes or a no, and a percentage indication as to who is keeping profitability and high touch goals, who isn't and to what degree (percentage). (See Appendix 14.)

The secondary manager's report is provided monthly. Some things to look for are:

(1) Are 95% of employee requests asking for recognition, respect or freedom, i.e., a form of touching?

(2) Are manager requests related to the corporate goals?
(3) Are both reviewer/employee keeping their agreements? What percentage of the time?
(4) Are all employees being reviewed?

## When Is Action Due?

(1) Managers' reports should be turned in monthly.
(2) Professional Growth Plan full-review meetings should be held every six months.
(3) Professional Growth Plan follow-up should be done every 90 days.
(4) Strategic planning sessions should be held annually, at the same time each year.
(5) One-on-one conferences should be held within 48 hours of a late follow-up sheet.

## Why Is All This Necessary?

(1) To be sure you will meet your goals and not get stuck in "Hope City."
(2) To heal your corporation and keep it growing, both financially and spiritually.
(3) To keep integrity alive and well in the corporation.
(4) To consistently break through addictive patterns by reducing the addict to *just one* request and to be up front with it.
(5) To consistently break through co-dependent patterns by forcing the co-dependent to come forward with *at least one* genuine request for themselves.

# 9

# Beyond Resistance

In the four main solutions already outlined (12-Step, planning, PGP, follow-up), we assume people are willing to improve. But because we have been testing these solutions for 10 years, we also assume that people resist change. So, no matter how charismatic the leader or how perfect the program, there is almost always resistance to improvement.

Resistance is often angry and reactive in areas that reveal an addictive or nonproductive behavior.

This is where gentleness comes in. Gently moving through the outlined stages is the key to dealing with resistance. The case of Jack, below, nicknamed "The Dictator" by his peers, shows us how even the worst case of resistance can be gently broken through.

### One Journey Beyond Resistance*

As chief consultant for a California firm, I signed a contract with Jack, general manager of a large manufac-

---

* This article was published as "Beyond Performance Review" by Mary Riley, Ph.D., in *Administrative Management*, March 1988, and is reprinted with permission from *Administrative Management*, copyright 1988, by Dalton Communications, Inc., New York.

turing corporation, to implement a Professional Growth
Plan system in his company. My assignment was to train
his top 60 managers in our system within three months.
What he didn't know (or, more likely, forgot) was that as
general manager he would do his PGP first. Jack said he
wanted to change but he fought it all the way.

Over the next several weeks, Jack missed all the
group sessions in which he was supposed to learn the
system. It became apparent to me that I would have to
schedule a special one-on-one session to teach him the
basics and to prepare him for his first review. Just like
his 60 managers, Jack would use numbers and a check-
off system for the first two steps of the review process.
I then acted as his partner for step 3, the funnel process.
I asked the required question: "What is the number one
thing you want from Paul (one of Jack's managers) to
make your job better?"

Jack immediately expressed his frustration with Paul
and complained about various aspects of Paul's work.

"He has no prototype," Jack said indignantly. "Paul
doesn't keep deadlines. He doesn't direct people. Last
week he didn't even acknowledge a due date. One time
he even . . ." on and on, Jack angrily complained.

I had heard this indignant, angry tone before. To me,
it is an indication that the funnel process is on track. The
goal is to help the manager move beyond indignation
and anger. Then he can, finally, explain clearly to another
individual what he wants done. For 15 minutes Jack
complained.

Finally, I pointed to the tip of the funnel sheet, stating,
"Jack, this is all a description of what you **don't** want.
Now tell me what you do want from Paul. In other
words, if you sent Paul to training camp and then he
came back to work, what would he be doing differently
than he does now?"

Jack got a sparkle in his eye as he made the miracu-
lous shift from anger to enlightenment. "Paul would
take a stand that productivity **will** increase," he said,
finally. He went on with enthusiasm. "In 30 days, Paul
would set up a prototype of vehicle assembly. He'd
videotape the prototype and show the video to the

employees. Then he'd write a productivity plan and stick to it."

On and on he went, bursting with all the knowledge and expectations he'd kept stored up in his own mind. He was quite unaware that he had never shared them with Paul — or anyone else for that matter. Jack was now ready for the third funnel question: "What would be different if Paul did all of this?" I asked.

"If he took a stand on higher productivity," Jack said, "and set up the prototype and made a plan, he'd reduce labor by 10%, materials by 5%."

I knew these were goals Jack had prepared four months earlier for every department. So far no one was achieving them.

To end our meeting and complete this part of the review process, Jack signed and dated our form. Meanwhile, Paul was preparing his PGP using the same process.

I was not present but I did learn that the number one thing Paul wanted from Jack was input on company goals.

Now Jack and Paul were prepared to meet face to face. Jack resisted. He was busy. He promised to get together with Paul in a few days. Two weeks went by. I sent him flowers with a note reminding him to meet with Paul.

"I will. I will," he said when I phoned. "This PGP process is great." But he didn't do it.

I sent a telegram to remind him. I kept calling. But he still didn't meet with Paul to do the review.

I knew Jack had brilliant insights to share with Paul. I couldn't stand to see them left unsaid. For the first time in ten years of consulting I decided to sit in on a review, just to be sure it would happen. Jack kept me waiting in an outer office while his final resistance crumbled. He knew I'd traveled 1,000 miles that day just to sit in on this session.

Finally face to face, Jack and Paul compared steps 1 and 2 without difficulty. The conversation was job-related and peaceful. In step 3 Jack was to ask Paul directly, "What is the number one thing you want from me, to make your job better?" He went rigid. He couldn't say the words. I had to ask the question for him.

"Paul, what is the number one thing you want from Jack to make your job better?"

"Input on goals," said Paul, clearly and with certainty.

"What!" declared Jack, ready to defend himself. "I have to get things done by certain dates given to me by corporate headquarters."

"Jack," I said firmly as I pressed on his arm, "our purpose here is to listen to Paul. Maybe he has other deadlines. Maybe he can't possibly meet one of yours. If he tells you that, you can both work on another solution. Our goal here is the truth."

What Jack did at that moment is probably the toughest thing for a human being to do — he purposefully gave up a long-held position and opened himself up to receive some new information. For 40 years he had been a leader issuing orders. He was not used to listening to followers. But he decided to listen to Paul. When the listening was over, he even made a commitment to let Paul have input on goals. Jack grumbled about participative management and complained about new ideas but he still wrote down his commitment to Paul and signed it.

Next, Jack told Paul what he wanted most from him. As a newly appointed vice-president, Paul had very little experience in leadership. Jack told Paul he wanted him to take a stand that productivity would increase. Paul's eyes lit up. I saw the same excitement Jack had experienced when he first identified the same need.

Paul reacted as though permission to succeed had been transferred to him. Until now, he had acted like a wimp. Now he had permission to be aggressive if it helped to meet production goals.

The two men agreed on their goals, thanked each other for a productive conversation and parted. In a week, I called Jack to see how he was doing on his commitment. He seemed irritated by my reminder but said he'd call back to report in a month. Thirty days later he was out of town.

Sixty days later I called Paul, "I'm calling," I said to Paul, "to see if Jack has kept his commitment about allowing your input on goals."

"Yes," said Paul. He seemed pleasantly surprised. "As a matter of fact, he has called me in twice to help set goals. But sometimes he goes back to his old dictator ways."

I was thrilled to hear that a hard core ex-military general manager could stretch even two times!

"Did you keep your commitment to Jack to take a stand to meet production goals?" I asked.

"I think so," said Paul. "At least I've tried."

A year later, other company sources told me that Paul had blossomed into a very good manager.

In reviewing the manager's report as part of the follow-up, we noticed that Jack had made the same request of each of his managers: Take a stand that productivity will increase. As a person, Jack embodied a stand for leadership and production. He wanted his team to hear his permission to be leaders too.

In Jack's struggle for communication, there are lessons for all of us. First, the thing we do best is often so natural that we don't know how to describe it. It makes us angry to try. Jack was a natural leader who had a long history of taking a stand. But he didn't realize that his own gift of leadership might not be natural to all those around him.

Second, many people need permission to act. For the most part, people don't assume they have permission. As a new manager, Paul was typical. Formerly an engineer, he was waiting for permission before taking command.

Third, it's hard for a nonlistener to learn to listen. It's tough to listen. And it takes courage.

Resistance is different for CEOs than it is for employees. Although both go through anger, enlightenment and high energy, employees are more likely to hold out for respect, recognition or freedom. Management wants support and cooperation.

Below, we have outlined the phases to be expected in shifting from addiction to productiveness. It's not an easy shift but understanding and staying focused during resistance is the key.

## Employees

The initial effect of increasing productivity in corporations has been, in our experience, a major eye-glazer with most groups of employees. We can be doing a seminar on any topic — communication, customer service, — but when the subject of increasing productivity comes up, we see four phases.

First, the attention instantly goes to anything other than increasing productivity. This has happened with public agencies, manufacturing companies, financial institutions, professional corporations, educational institutions and nonprofit agencies. We have even noticed glazed *ears* on the phone. If we are discussing this issue with the CEO's secretary, as soon as the secretary hears "increase productivity," they often think this is a request for faster typing, more filing or longer hours and the glaze in the secretary's voice suddenly says *Oh . . . er . . . she'll call if she's interested.*

One CEO's secretary gave signs of being mentally absent from the moment we mentioned productivity. Seeming to want to get rid of us, she said, "I'll tell him about it and he'll call if he's interested." We couldn't resist the temptation of asking "What are you going to tell him about us?" She hesitated and then said in an indignant tone, "That you are a head hunter!"

"But we aren't," I protested, "we are . . ."

"Well, whatever you are, he's not interested," she said. "Good-bye," and she hung up.

## CEOs, Owners And Directors

The same glaze appears in the eyes of CEOs, owners and directors except over different subjects. They glaze in response to such issues as: helping employees, training, recognition and better listening skills for employees. We saw an example of this in a meeting with a CEO in a major U.S. city. We were directed by the mayor to call the CEO's attention to an employee grievance about department heads' apathy toward employee equal rights issues. He fell asleep during the meeting.

Another time, I was in the process of signing a contract for a Professional Growth Plan with the president of a large aerospace company. In our presentation, we had zeroed in on how this PGP would directly increase productiveness and morale simultaneously. I noticed the president's glazed eyes when we said "morale." As he signed the contract the next week he said, "Now this will help us comply with EEO law, right?" It was as if he never absorbed the idea that people could really be a source of increased productivity; the PGP was just another irritating compliance issue to him.

## Anger

### Employees

Anger is usually the phase after the glaze (no rhyme intended). The secretary in the above case spoke for many employees who feel that more and more work is heaped on them with no compensation for the increase. In many cases they are right. Corporations without clearly defined goals see deadlines coming and ask employees to rush to meet them. By not scheduling, planning and organizing properly, managers create the crunch. Rather than take responsibility for not planning properly, managers project the problem on to employees. So there is clearly some justification for the angry responses from employees.

But another employee response that is not justifiable, in our opinion, is the negative reaction when it is suggested that increasing productivity might reveal or uncover nonproductiveness. Anger is a way for employees to keep everyone away so they won't be found out. There is a strong possibility that there are some addictive processes going on because of their evident focus on something other than productiveness. A specific example of this was the union example and the faculty group mentioned earlier.

With the faculty group, at the first seminar half of the people were on time, a fourth were an average of 30 minutes late and a fourth never showed. The addiction of the last two groups to obsession with items other than quality education and their codependence on others' addictions was close to being exposed — their avoidance only made that more obvious.

The president first wrote on the board, "The number one goal of this college for the next five years is to improve the quality of education for students." The group went to phase one — the glazed look. We do not believe they heard anything the president said about the board giving this direction . . . "The board represents the community . . . we are here to serve the community . . ." etc.

"This is a personal affront," said one participant. "This says we don't have quality education and I say we do." Everyone cheered.

Another said, "We're so busy with day-to-day crises we don't have a chance to take on one more issue." The group demanded that each person tell how overwhelmed he was with meetings, problems, teaching classes and administrative responsibilities. They criticized the board, the college, the president, the seminar and the students. Two or three were silent. Not one indicated a willingness to accept the challenge of improving the quality of education.

In another example, a key person co-dependent manufacturing company designed a mission statement, set goals and contracted to train managers and supervisors on the goals and the mission.

Managers and supervisors became excited about their ability to zero in on the corporate profit goal and to identify ways to increase it. Because this was a key person co-dependent corporation, it was filled with employees who were hungry for goals and deadlines. They wanted structure. They wanted to see achievable results. With high touch achieved, this group was ready for high tech.

Meanwhile, we had lost sight of some of the issues of the kind and loving president/owner of the company. He had been delaying buying automated equipment because it was to come out of his own savings, as owner. Anger was building in this president after employees asked him to purchase the new automated technology.

Given his co-dependent nature, he always did things for everyone else and then felt infuriated by a request for more money to buy things. He blew up and walked out, saying, "This makes me angry." In the three months that followed, he never did tell anyone why he was angry or that the incident even occurred.

The anger in this case was directed at the employees — because if you sacrifice everything for your employees, which he did — there is a boiling point. An honest look at his anger would allow him to see the co-dependency he had with employees. Never wanting to hurt them or push them or confront them, had taken its toll. The resolution was in healing the co-dependency, not in fury at an employee request.

Beyond his anger, he would see that employees were truly committed to the company. Many CEOs never see this.

### Enlightenment And High Energy

#### Employees/Employers

The third phase in shifting to productivity out of addictiveness is one of enlightenment. Enlightenment turns to high energy so quickly that we are merging the title and examples. The link between boss and employee is renewed and strong.

During enlightenment, employees discover that (1) they will personally benefit from contributing to the corporate goals, (2) they are the best ones to do their own jobs, and (3) they are a key part of the goals. They experience joy and balance when they proceed toward productive goals. For employers, enlightenment offers a chance to see that they are not alone — they are not the only ones who care about profit. They discover a connection between listening to employees' ideas and being more profitable.

We are now ready to continue the story of the manufacturing company mentioned in the Anger section. After the president calmed down, he was asked what his employees could do to support him. It had never dawned on him earlier that his employees were committed to his company's success. He just thought the automation request was made out of selfishness and greed. The funnel process discussed earlier was a tool that led him to shift from anger at the employees' demand to enlightenment about the support they gave him. He had requests. He wanted the controller to provide him with more cash flow information and to make more decisions. From the vice-president of engineering, he requested six new products a year. He asked the executive vice-president to "chart the course — tell me what's out there in the field." From sales, he wanted a higher quota.

He told his vice-president of manufacturing to implement a manual inventory production control system. He began to detail what that system would look like and what it would do. As he talked, he discovered the need for it to be automated. Now he, the president, had become enlightened. He saw the need for automation if sales were to increase as forecasted and if six new products were to be developed and if manufacturing was to keep up with sales.

Supervisors in the manufacturing group were also becoming a very motivated group. They jumped right into the process of shifting from their complaints (no goals, too much chaos, no commitment from top management) to their managers' requests. Four of these requests from supervisors were:

(1) Give me direction and a way to measure my employees.
(2) Let me know how I am doing. Meet every Wednesday at 9:00 A.M. for 15 minutes to discuss what's working or not working in my job.
(3) Help me plan, organize and schedule. Give me a sample schedule and check on it weekly to see if it's as efficient as it could be.
(4) Delegate more authority to me. Let me handle personnel issues in my department.

Each of these four requests, if met, would result in increased productivity in the end.

The next week the supervisors found out what their managers' one goal was. This common goal was requested separately by most managers of their supervisors and was generated by the newly enlightened president. The goal was: Assist in implementing the manual inventory production control system.

Each manager broke down his or her request into specific parts for each supervisor. For example, one supervisor was to have a 48-hour turnaround time from receiving the sales order to having the item on the production line. Another supervisor was to make sure all working drawings in engineering matched the machinery that would be building it, e.g., right to left, or vice-versa if the machine went from left to right.

For four weeks the supervisors aligned their requests with the managers' requests. Then they diligently prepared a speech on exactly how their goal would be achieved and what would be the measure of success.

The speeches were a shock to a management team who had kept these supervisors in subordinate roles, rarely asking for their input.

The energy in the room was happy and creative as the managers sat in awe of supervisors excited about goals, thinking about them, talking about them, listening to how they all fit with one another's. The joy of coming together in this manner transcends any addictive substance or process. It is really the high we are each looking for but sometimes forget how to get.

So our contention is that the best thing an organization can do to break through nonproductive energies is to use a system (we recommend PGP) to break through resistance and refocus on goals. Only then can we move beyond the glaze, beyond the anger and on to enlightenment and high energy. Being productive is the basis for high morale. We can't wait for high morale and say *Then we'll be productive*. Productiveness creates high morale.

# 10

# How Do We Start?

The corporation exists to make profit. The number one thing the corporation needs from all employees is to support that profit goal.

Employees want to be respected as individuals. If they are given a chance to tell how they want that respect and it is granted, they will support the profit goals.

When the corporation respects individual employees according to their requests and the employees support the profit goal, there is a healing corporation.

If you support the profit goal 100% and respect the employees' requests 100%, you do not need to do another thing.

If you do not support the profit goal 100% or if you do not respect employees' requests 100%, then you may start by admitting you have made some mistakes. Admit you have not been taking care of corporate health as well as you could.

If you tend toward the key person addict traits, admit this: I have not been in touch with what my people need in order to support the profit goal. I have been in Hope City hoping they were committed to profit. I thought I knew but I do not truly know, how to show those reporting directly to me the respect they would like. The impact of my not being in touch with people has increased their reliance on addictive activities.

If you tend toward key person co-dependent traits admit this: I have not acted out of a true commitment to the profit goals of this company. I get sidetracked by wanting to be liked and not to upset people. While I pretended that the training, the new computer program, the counseling and/or helping others was going to help profit, I was really in Hope City and did not go the extra distance to link my work to profitability. The impact of my co-dependency has been to waste company money and thus decrease the profit we could have made.

Join a 12-Step program so you can open your mind to possibility and understand the massive healing process that so many people are working on all over the county. If you have an addiction try AA or a similar group. If you are co-dependent find a suitable group. Commit to a minimum of ten consecutive sessions.

Read your corporate profit goals and make sure you understand them and your responsibility to them. If you are a CEO or executive, set out to hire a Vice-President of Corporate Vision. If you are not a CEO, find out the number one item your supervisor wants from you.

Schedule a strategic planning session as soon as possible. If you don't have the authority, strongly request it of your CEO. They may resist at first but may be very appreciative later.

Implement the Professional Growth Plan as quickly as possible after you have formed the company goals. Even if you supervise only one person, it will be a benefit. Clarify the goal to that person. Find out what he wants in return. Don't ask — funnel!

Use the planning follow-up with great accuracy and intention. People will see that these commitments are for real and respond enthusiastically and keep on responding.

Work continually on clearing up your own addictive/co-dependent tendencies. Like diet and exercise, it is a lifelong project with a major positive impact.

# 11

# Summary

During the 1960s, '70s and '80s, a separation occurred between the individual and the corporation. There are three main reasons for this: (1) the divisive effect of the Vietnam conflict, (2) the high technology era, which depersonalized the workplace and (3) the escalation of substance abuse, particularly illegal drugs.

People have fallen into addictive behaviors at an alarmingly increasing rate. Many corporations are losing money and plummeting into major debt because of this.

This book calls upon us to confront the addictive behaviors that affect 96% of our population. Nonproductive/addictive activities have penetrated the corporate world. But rather than addressing ourselves to placating people, we would remind the reader of the value that productiveness can hold for both the individual and the corporation.

We reviewed historic and legal aspects, as well as current research.

We examined the stages of resistance that might be expected if we are to merge the individual with the corporation: boredom, anger, enlightenment and finally, increased energy.

We examined Either/Or Thinking — either it's for the corporation or it's for the individual. Perhaps our new concept, corporate healing, could encompass both.

As President Bush, in his Inaugural Address, asked that we unite our two cultures from the 1960s, we ask, could we not consider uniting the individual and the corporation and have a stronger and more caring corporation in the 1990s? We believe such a union would help free the individual from addictive behaviors, while helping the corporation to become more profitable.

If each individual will take responsibility for his or her own unproductive habits and if the corporation will begin touching the individual with respect, then the healing process will begin. The goal is a healthy corporation. A healthy corporation is one that respects the individual according to that individual's request. In turn, the individual actively supports the corporation.

# Chapter Notes

## Chapter 1

1. Schaef, Anne Wilson and Fassel, Diane, **Addictive Organizations**, New York: Harper & Row, 1988.
2. A 1980 Xerox Learning Systems study showed that the #1 complaint of employees is lack of recognition.
3. Lowen, Alexander, M.D., **Narcissism, Denial Of The True Self**. New York: Macmillan, 1985.

## Chapter 2

1. Robinson, Bryan, E., **Work Addiction: Hidden Legacies Of Adult Children**. Deerfield Beach, FL: Health Communications, 1989.

## Chapter 3

1. Peck, M. Scott, M.D., **People of the Lie**. New York: Simon & Schuster, 1983.

## Chapter 4

1. Perkins, Rollin and Boyce, Ronald, **Criminal Law and Procedure**, Vol. VI, p. 17. New York: Foundation Press, 1984.

2. Durant, Will and Ariel, **A Dual Autobiography**. New York: Simon & Schuster, 1977.

## Chapter 5

1. Bradshaw, John, **Bradshaw On: The Family**. Deerfield Beach, FL: Health Communications, 1988.
2. Miller, Keith, **Sin: Overcoming the Ultimate Addiction**. New York: Harper & Row, 1987.
3. Pinchott, Gifford III, **Intrapreneuring**. New York: Harper & Row, 1985.

# APPENDIX 1

## RECOGNITION*

| (SUPPOSEDLY POSITIVE) | POSITIVE | (ACTUALLY POSITIVE) |
| A | ↑ | B |

**ADDICTIVE**

Column A:
Do you need more time off?

How are you coming with your AA program?

Did your aunt recover from her surgery?

How's the non-smoking going?

What did your ex do now?

Column B:
I like the way you solved that technical problem without blaming anyone.

I noticed you were very quick with those answers today.

We made the deadline. Thanks.

Good job on detailing in paragraph form how you got those numbers.

Your report was clear, short and powerful.

UNHEALTHY UNPRODUCTIVE ← → HEALTHY PRODUCTIVE

**CO-DEPENDENT**

Column C:
You aren't analytical enough.

You blew it.

You will never be a manager.

You're too stubborn.

You never read the instructions.

You have a poor attitude.

Column D:
We missed the deadline. Let's reschedule.

There are four typos in this report.

We lost the King account.

The figures did not add up on this report.

Our client said they never received an evaluation form that was promised them.

| C | ↓ | D |
| (ACTUALLY NEGATIVE) | NEGATIVE | (SUPPOSEDLY NEGATIVE) |

*Taking notice in some definite way.     ©Morgan Research & Innovation

107

# APPENDIX 2

## Basic 12-Step Program

1. We admitted we were powerless over alcohol — that our lives had become unmanageable.

2. Came to believe that a Power greater than ourselves could restore us to sanity.

3. Made a decision to turn our will and our lives over to the care of God as we understood Him.

4. Made a searching and fearless moral inventory of ourselves.

5. Admitted to God, to ourselves and to another human being the exact nature of our wrongs.

6. Were entirely ready to have God remove all these defects of character.

7. Humbly asked Him to remove our shortcomings.

8. Made a list of all persons we had harmed and became willing to make amends to them all.

9. Made direct amends to such people whenever possible except when to do so would injure them or others.

10. Continued to take personal inventory and when we were wrong, promptly admitted it.

11. Sought through prayer and meditation to improve our conscious contact with God as we understood Him, praying only for knowledge of His will for us and the power to carry that out.

12. Having had a spiritual awakening as the result of these Steps, we tried to carry this message to alcoholics and to practice these principles in all our affairs.

# APPENDIX 3

## 12 -Step Program In The Workplace

1. We admitted we were powerless over [ *whatever addiction* ] and our productiveness has decreased because of it.

2. We came to accept that we do not currently know everything we could know about our jobs.

3. We made a decision to accept the guidance of one other in the organization who is more familiar with the job.

4. We made a searching and fearless moral inventory of ourselves.

5. We admitted to ourselves and to another human being the exact nature of our sabotaging behavior on the job.

6. We were entirely ready to listen to the guidance and, for a moment, to let go of our original viewpoint.

7. Acknowledged the guidance, summarized it; asked questions to further understand it; said "thank you" and agreed to undertake the suggestion.

8. Made a list of all the persons we had harmed and became willing to make amends to them, to others or to the corporation.

9. Made direct amends to such people whenever possible except when to do so would injure them or others.

10. Continued to take personal inventory and when we were wrong, promptly admitted it.

11. We are now safe to let our entrepreneurial spirit come back to life.

12. Having recaptured our entrepreneurial spirit, we carried this message to others whom we saw imprisoned in resistance to their own productiveness and creativity.

# APPENDIX 4

## Professional Growth Plan Meeting Agenda

Employee and reviewer are scheduled to hold a Professional Growth Plan meeting soon. This review method has been customized for your company's use. To prepare for this review, you should do the following:

1. Read all of the information on this sheet and on the Pre-Review forms.
2. Fill out the reviewer's Pre-Review form (both pages).
3. Set a time to hold the review. (If this is your first review, the meeting will last about an hour.)
4. Bring your copy of the Pre-Review form to the Professional Growth Plan Meeting.
5. Conduct the Professional Growth Plan Meeting. Complete the Alignment sheet and *both* sign it. See step #3 as outlined below.

The Professional Growth Plan session will follow four steps:

### Step 1 — Discussing skills that are important to the employee's job

Compare items the reviewer numbered in Section I with the numbers that the employee marked in Section I. Where there is a difference in rating, mark the other person's number in the margin. Do not ask or expect the other to change his/her number — do take note of his viewpoint.

### Step 2 — Discussing the job skills the employee performs well

Compare items in Section II. Where one party has an X but the other does not, make a note in the margin. For every X reviewer has on his form, tell the employee, specifically, why you think he/she does particularly well in this skill. Cite an example. Employee Xs are acknowledged in margin of reviewer's form.

**Step 3 — Alternately disclose requests** (the item you prepared in Section III)

Take out the Alignment sheet and fill in your name and the date. Please print.

Employee's #1 request will become Goal #1. Reviewer asks the employee for his or her #1 request. Discuss it until you agree. Alter it if necessary. Write it in under Goal #1 on the Alignment sheet. Next, write out three verbs under "How Achieved" to describe your picture of what the reviewer would do to achieve this goal. Complete the "How Measured" section telling what would be different if the goal were achieved.

Now the Alignment sheet goes to the employee. Reviewer tells the employee the request prepared on reviewer Pre-Review sheet. Employee writes out the main point on the Alignment sheet under Goal #2.

Repeat for Goal #3 (Employee Request) and #4 (Reviewer Request).

**Step 4 — Commitment to one another's requests**

Both of you sign and date the Alignment sheet and immediately send a copy to _____. In 90 days you will both be asked if the goals/requests were met.

# APPENDIX 5

## Professional Growth Plan
### Pre-Review

Organization: _____  Date: _____

Employee Name (Print): _____  Reviewer Name (Print): _____

Employee's Position: _____

## Step I

**Instructions:** Please indicate in column "Importance To Job" whether the category is 3 — "Most Important"; 2 — "Important"; 1 — "Less Important" or 0 — "Not Applicable". You can only use the rating of "3" five times. No limit on 0, 1 or 2.

# Professional Growth Plan Cont. – Step I

## JOB SKILLS

| IMPORTANCE TO JOB 3, 2, 1, 0 | PERFORMANCE CATEGORIES |
|---|---|
| | 1. USING OPERATING POLICIES PRESCRIBED FOR THE JOB |
| | 2. MEETING COMPANY GOALS, OBJECTIVES AND COMMITMENTS |
| | 3. USING TIME EFFICIENTLY/EFFECTIVELY |
| | 4. FOLLOWING THROUGH ON TASKS AND ACTIVITIES |
| | 5. APPLYING TECHNICAL KNOWLEDGE |
| | 6. GENERATING NEW IDEAS AND SUGGESTIONS (INITIATIVE) |
| | 7. MEETING DEADLINES |
| | 8. EFFECTIVELY COMMUNICATING WITH OTHERS |
| | 9. MAKING TIMELY DECISIONS, JUDGMENTS |
| | 10. SEEING A JOB TO COMPLETION |
| | 11. SOLVING JOB-RELATED PROBLEMS |
| | 12. MAINTAINING EFFECTIVE WORK RELATIONS WITH CO-WORKERS (TEAMWORK, ATTITUDE) |
| | 13. PROVIDING QUALITY SERVICE, PUBLIC CONTACT SKILLS |
| | 14. ORGANIZING, PLANNING AND SCHEDULING OF WORK |
| | 15. SAFETY (WORK AREA, EQUIPMENT) |
| | 16. ATTENDANCE, PUNCTUALITY, AVAILABILITY |
| | 17. PROPER OPERATION AND CARE OF EQUIPMENT |
| | 18. |
| | 19. |

114

# Professional Growth Plan Cont. – Step II

PUT 5 Xs TO MARK SKILLS EMPLOYEE PERFORMS BEST.

## JOB SKILLS

| EMPLOYEE DOES BEST | PERFORMANCE CATEGORIES | | | | |
|---|---|---|---|---|---|
| 3, 2, 1, 0 | | | | | |
| | 1. USING OPERATING POLICIES PRESCRIBED FOR THE JOB | | | | |
| | 2. MEETING COMPANY GOALS, OBJECTIVES AND COMMITMENTS | | | | |
| | 3. USING TIME EFFICIENTLY/EFFECTIVELY | | | | |
| | 4. FOLLOWING THROUGH ON TASKS AND ACTIVITIES | | | | |
| | 5. APPLYING TECHNICAL KNOWLEDGE | | | | |
| | 6. GENERATING NEW IDEAS AND SUGGESTIONS (INITIATIVE) | | | | |
| | 7. MEETING DEADLINES | | | | |
| | 8. EFFECTIVELY COMMUNICATING WITH OTHERS | | | | |
| | 9. MAKING TIMELY DECISIONS, JUDGMENTS | | | | |
| | 10. SEEING A JOB TO COMPLETION | | | | |
| | 11. SOLVING JOB-RELATED PROBLEMS | | | | |
| | 12. MAINTAINING EFFECTIVE WORK RELATIONS WITH CO-WORKERS (TEAMWORK, ATTITUDE) | | | | |
| | 13. PROVIDING QUALITY SERVICE, PUBLIC CONTACT SKILLS | | | | |
| | 14. ORGANIZING, PLANNING AND SCHEDULING OF WORK | | | | |
| | 15. SAFETY (WORK AREA, EQUIPMENT) | | | | |
| | 16. ATTENDANCE, PUNCTUALITY, AVAILABILITY | | | | |
| | 17. PROPER OPERATION AND CARE OF EQUIPMENT | | | | |
| | 18. | | | | |
| | 19. | | | | |

# Employee's Pre-Review (page 2)

## Step III. Stating Requests

How can your reviewer make your job better for you? List three (3) things your reviewer could do that would help make you be more productive in your work. Remember that an effective goal is realistic, specific and has a date. After each request, use three verbs in the "How Achieved" question to describe how *you* want this done. Be clear.

---

**SAMPLE:** REQUEST #1: __Give me more responsibility.__

HOW IS THIS GOAL TO BE ACHIEVED? __Put me in charge of data output, let me set a schedule,__

__refer any questions on data input to me.__

HOW AND WHEN WILL PROGRESS BE MEASURED? __Errors would drop to two per week.__

EXPECTED DATE FOR ACCOMPLISHING THIS ITEM? __December 1, 1990__

REQUEST #1: _____

HOW IS THIS TO BE ACHIEVED? _____

HOW WILL PROGRESS BE MEASURED? _____

EXPECTED DATE FOR ACCOMPLISHING THIS ITEM? _____

REQUEST #2: _____

HOW IS THIS TO BE ACHIEVED? _____

HOW WILL PROGRESS BE MEASURED? _____

EXPECTED DATE FOR ACCOMPLISHING THIS ITEM? _____

REQUEST #3: _____

HOW IS THIS TO BE ACHIEVED? _____

HOW WILL PROGRESS BE MEASURED? _____

EXPECTED DATE FOR ACCOMPLISHING THIS ITEM? _____

# Reviewer's Pre-Review (page 2)

Note to reviewer: Wherever you had a "3" written in Section I (eg. _3_ 10.) but there is not an "X" in Section II by that same skill, place a dot above the line (eg. . _ 10). Of the skills with a dot, select the most important to you and write it below under Section III Request #1. Continue for Request #2 and Request #3. If you had no dots, think: What would you like from this employee that would make your job better for you? Remember that an effective request is realistic, specific and has a date.

## Step III. Stating Requests

With these thoughts in mind, state the three (3) things you want from this employee in order for your job to be more productive for you. After each request, use three verbs in the "How Achieved" question to describe your picture of how you want this done. Be clear.

---

**SAMPLE:** REQUEST #1:   Take action to meet deadlines.

HOW IS THIS GOAL TO BE ACHIEVED?   Make a list, prioritize, draw a wall chart
and update it daily.

HOW AND WHEN WILL PROGRESS BE MEASURED?   Wall chart will always have current
dates. We will meet 90% of our deadlines.

EXPECTED DATE FOR ACCOMPLISHING THIS ITEM?   December 1, 1990

---

REQUEST #1: _____

HOW IS THIS TO BE ACHIEVED? _____

HOW WILL PROGRESS BE MEASURED? _____

EXPECTED DATE FOR ACCOMPLISHING THIS ITEM? _____

REQUEST #2: _____

HOW IS THIS TO BE ACHIEVED? _____

HOW WILL PROGRESS BE MEASURED? _____

EXPECTED DATE FOR ACCOMPLISHING THIS ITEM? _____

REQUEST #3: _____

HOW IS THIS TO BE ACHIEVED? _____

HOW WILL PROGRESS BE MEASURED? _____

EXPECTED DATE FOR ACCOMPLISHING THIS ITEM? _____

# APPENDIX 6

## The Distinction Between Performance Reviews And The Professional Growth Plan

TYPE A PERFORMANCE REVIEW

- Analytical paragraph style written by supervisor
- Supervisor in judgmental position
- Subjective on part of supervisor
- Emphasizes strengths and weaknesses of the employee
- Minimal employee input
- No mutual goal setting

TYPE B PERFORMANCE REVIEW

- Report card where supervisor rates employee in key areas
- Subjective on part of supervisor
- Points out weaknesses and strengths of the employee
- Minimal employee input
- No mutual goal setting

TYPE C PERFORMANCE REVIEW

- Encourages goal setting but guidelines are rarely followed
- Judges the employee
- Goals usually set by supervisor for employee
- Employee input is oriented toward what the boss wants
- Goal setting is supposed to be mutual but employee's touch needs do not show up

PROFESSIONAL GROWTH PLAN

- Increased profit results as employee touch needs and corporate productivity needs are simultaneously provided.
- Discusses job skills employee performs well — builds on employee strengths.
- Gives employee positive feedback and recognition.
- Nets out what employee really wants in the job so his/her "touch" request will be granted.
- Aligns goals — each agrees to support what the other wants for the job to be better. Each contributes to goals that are in line with company's objectives.
- Follow-up provides regular feedback on how well employee is doing on profit goals.
- Eliminates many opportunites for addictive and co-dependent behavior.

# APPENDIX 7

Name: _____

Date: _____

Funneler: _____

## Goal: Stated In Positive Terms, The Number One Item I Want Is:

SPECIFICALLY —
WHAT IT
WOULD LOOK LIKE.
(How is this to be
  achieved?)

WHAT SPECIFICALLY
WOULD
BE DIFFERENT.
(How will progress
  be measured?)

Date to begin: _____

Date completed (Checked): _____

# APPENDIX 8

## Most Common Employee Requests

| WHAT DO YOU WANT? | WHAT WOULD IT LOOK LIKE? | WHAT WOULD BE DIFFERENT? | WHEN SHOULD IT HAPPEN? |
|---|---|---|---|
| 1. More responsibility | A. Put me in charge of the data processing input section. B. Let me call for repairs. C. Let me train the new person. | Errors would drop below two per week. | By August 3 |
| 2. More independence. | A. Tell me the goal you want, then trust me to do it my way. B. Let me know my budget. | I'd get production out on time. | By January 15 |
| 3. Give me more recognition. | A. Tell me when I have done a good job handling a customer complaint. B. Let me know if a customer tells you they are pleased. C. Include my name on the report I wrote. | I'll know the standard and thus satisfy customers sooner. You'll get no more than one complaint per month. | By June 15 |
| 4. Maintain better communications with me. | A. Meet with me every Wednesday 9:00-9:15 in your office. B. Discuss my job. C. Let me know how I'm doing. | I'd get work done sooner. I'd have time to work on the emergency plan. | By January 15 |

| | | | |
|---|---|---|---|
| 5. Supply me with more training. | A. Teach me more about our new rental equipment. B. Send me to the course at the local college. C. Get an extra manual for me. | I'd be more efficient with the equipment — able to explain its use to others. | By March 1 |
| 6. Let me have input on goals. | A. When you write out bi-annual department goals for my department, let's do it together. B. Ask me what timeline I see as realistic. C. Let me review them before they are published. | I'll reach all my goals. | By July 3 |
| 7. Go through the chain of command. | A. Talk to me prior to discussing problems or requests with my project members. B. If one of my employees comes to you with a problem, send them to me. C. If you do make agreements with them, let me know. | I can measure progress on an ongoing basis with my knowledge of project members' activity. We can get the product under budget and on time. | By May 17 |
| 8. Keep me informed. | A. Keep me more informed on division and company wide business. B. Let me attend the monthly meeting. C. Give me a copy of any memos affecting my department. | I'd meet deadlines. | By February 1 |

©Morgan Research & Innovation 1989

123

# APPENDIX 9

## Most Common Manager Requests

| WHAT DO YOU WANT? | WHAT WOULD IT LOOK LIKE: | WHAT WOULD BE DIFFERENT? | WHEN SHOULD IT HAPPEN? |
|---|---|---|---|
| 1. Motivate and develop your staff. | A. Set clear goals. B. Find out what each needs from you to reach those goals and commit to their request. C. Follow through — acknowledge where they are every three days and reward for accomplishments. Reschedule if not achieved. | We would decrease turnover from 40% to 20%. | By February 1 |
| 2. Keep track of materials. | A. Inventory your materials every day. B. Request needed materials at least three days before you run out. C. Lock your materials cabinet when you leave the office. | Would be able to support the needs of the managers to get the product out the door 24 hours before deadline. | By February 15 |
| 3. Socialize only during your lunch hours and break. | A. Remain at your work station during business hours. B. Talk only business on the telephone. C. Talk about business-related issues only. | 25% more transactions weekly. | By January 15 |

| | | | |
|---|---|---|---|
| 4. Clean up your work station before you leave at night. | A. Put floormat in place. B. Wipe down work station. C. Put tools in tool box. | Be ready to begin machines by 7:00 a.m. | By January 22 |
| 5. A. Let me know about problems in your work before they become crises. | A. Give me a weekly report on any problems you see in your work area. B. Give me recommendations to solve your problems. C. Follow through on solutions to problems. | No union grievances. | By January 31 |
| 6. Prioritize your tasks. | A. Meet with me once a week, Monday 8:00 a.m. B. Give to me each Friday 4:00 p.m. list of weekly accomplishments. C. Ask me if you get confused on priorities. | Inventory would have a 24 hour turnaround. | By January 15 |

©Morgan Research & Innovation 1989

# APPENDIX 10

Please print:                          Review Date _____
Employee's Name _____    Checkpoint Date _____
Reviewer's Name _____    Organization _____

## Professional Growth Plan Agreement (Alignment Sheet)

Below you will merge Reviewer and Employee goals and requests. Each of you will write the request of the other as clear and concise as possible. Be sure you agree to the item before writing it. When complete, sign and date this form at the bottom.

**Employee Request** (To be written by Reviewer)

GOAL #1: _____

How is this goal to be achieved? _____

How and when will progress be measured? _____

Expected date for beginning/completing this goal? _____

**Reviewer Goal** (To be written by Employee)

GOAL #2: _____

How is this goal to be achieved? _____

How and when will progress be measured? _____

Expected date for beginning/completing this goal? _____

**Employee Request** (To be written by Reviewer)

GOAL #3: _____

How is this goal to be achieved? _____

How and when will progress be measured? _____

Expected date for beginning/completing this goal? _____

**Reviewer Goal** (To be written by Employee)

GOAL #4: _____

How is this goal to be achieved? _____

How and when will progress be measured? _____

Expected date for beginning/completing this goal? _____

_____          _____
Reviewer's Signature    Date    Employee's Signature    Date

126

# APPENDIX 11
# SAMPLE

Please print:
Employee's Name _____
Reviewer's Name _____

Review Date _____
Checkpoint Date _____
Organization _____

## Professional Growth Plan Agreement (Alignment Sheet)

Below you will merge Reviewer and Employee goals and requests. Each of you will write the request of the other as clear and concise as possible. Be sure you agree to the item before writing it. When complete, sign and date this form at the bottom.

**Employee Request** (To be written by Reviewer)

GOAL #1: Let me have input on goals.

How is this goal to be achieved? Ask me which date I think we can reach deadline, include me in goal related meetings, tell me results.

How and when will progress be measured? Deadlines will have integrity and will be met 80% of the time.

Expected date for beginning/completing this goal? June 2 — September 2

**Reviewer Goal** (To be written by Employee)

GOAL #2: Take action to lead your employees to meeting goals.

How is this goal to be achieved? Meet weekly, assign responsibilities, make a wall chart, monitor all goals, call them on it if they don't meet deadlines.

How and when will progress be measured? A wallchart will exist and always have current dates. We'll meet our monthly production goals and in October and November surpass them.

Expected date for beginning/completing this goal? June 2 — July 2

**Employee Request** (To be written by Reviewer)

GOAL #3: Give me the freedom to manage my own way.

How is this goal to be achieved? Tell me the result you want, then let me get there on my own. Let me make and correct my own mistakes.

How and when will progress be measured? I will be asking you questions on how to do things — goals will be met — 90% of deliveries will be on time.

Expected date for beginning/completing this goal? June 2 — July 2

**Reviewer Goal** (To be written by Employee)

GOAL #4: Meet more delivery deadlines. Increase from 81% to 90%.

How is this goal to be achieved? Hold your employees accountable for dates. When even one date slips, acknowledge the error and correct the problem.

How and when will progress be measured? 90% deliveries completed for August.

Expected date for beginning/completing this goal? August 1 — September 1

_____    _____    _____    _____
Reviewer's Signature             Date       Employee's Signature          Date

# APPENDIX 12

**Professional Growth Plan
Follow-Up System**

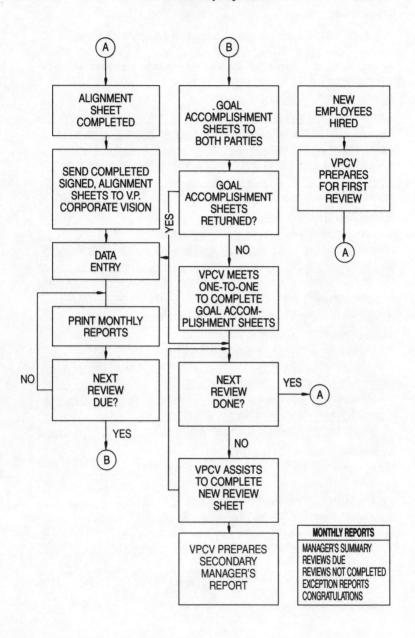

# APPENDIX 13

## Manager's Primary Report

| Reviewer | Employee Name | Date | Employee Request | Emp. % | Rev. % | Reviewer Request | Emp. % | Rev. % |
|---|---|---|---|---|---|---|---|---|
| A | a | | Work with me to finalize my responsibilities | | | Meet deadlines | | |
| | b | | Reset my % chargeable time to 85%, outside of tax season | | | To assist firm in client development | | |
| | c | | Continued responsibility | | | Give me more feedback on client status | | |
| | d | | Client responsibility/managing the account | | | Make practice development a part of your job | | |

# APPENDIX 14

## Manager's Secondary Report

| Reviewer | Employee Name | Date | Employee Request | Emp. % | Rev. % | Reviewer Request | Emp. % | Rev. % |
|---|---|---|---|---|---|---|---|---|
| A | a | | Delegate more responsibility | 25% | 40% | Take charge of clients and related work | 60% | 60% |
| | b | | Completed product to client by due date | 60% | 70% | Make notes re assignments | 70% | 75% |
| | c | | List of procedures and checklists | 90% | 90% | Inform me of time availability | 80% | 40% |
| B | d | | Brainstorm w/me once a month for speaking engagements | 80% | 60% | Actively support profit goals | 50% | 50% |
| | e | | Complete job scheduling through revenue budget stage | 20% | 40% | Follow through on practice development commitments | 30% | 80% |
| C | f | | Responsibility for decisions for AP | 50% | 60% | Schedule work | 90% | 80% |
| | g | | Manage accounts and more responsibility | 80% | 80% | Take more responsibility for clients | 100% | 100% |

# APPENDIX 15

## Job Description

TITLE: Vice-President for Corporate Vision

MISSION: Keeper of the Corporate Vision

EDUCATON REQUIRED:

MBA or Divinity degree from an accredited university.

EXPERIENCE:

1. Ten years of corporate supervisory or managerial experience in areas of operations, finance, marketing, labor relations or systems.
2. Five years of corporate executive level experience.
3. Three years experience as an employee in an hourly job (part-time is acceptable).
4. Five years of ministry experience may be substituted for half of the ten years in #1 above.

DUTIES:

1. Conduct 12-Step Program In The Workplace meetings.
2. Conduct Strategic Planning Sessions.
3. Conduct Professional Growth Plan seminars.
   A. Customize Forms.
   B. Implement a system for reminders and upkeep.
4. Monitor Follow-Up program.
5. Present monthly Secondary Reports to president and executive staff.

HOURS AND TIMELINE:

The Vice-President for Corporate Vision cannot be at the corporate facility more than 30 hours per week.

The job is only valid for one year.

The VPCV is to be included in all executive sessions.

SALARY:

Salary shall be the average of all other Vice-Presidents' salaries.

# APPENDIX 16

## Goal Accomplishment Questionnaire

Please print:    Date: _____    To: _____

Employee's Name: _____    Reviewer's Name _____

Goal #1: _____

Was Goal #1 Accomplished?    Yes ____ %    No ____    If No, Explain: _____

_____

Was Goal #2 Accomplished?    Yes ____ %    No ____    If No, Explain: _____

_____

Was Goal #3 Accomplished?    Yes ____ %    No ____    If No, Explain: _____

_____

Was Goal #4 Accomplished?    Yes ____ %    No ____    If No, Explain: _____

_____

# Bibliography

Beattie, Melody. **Co-dependent No More: How to Stop Controlling Others and Start Caring For Yourself.** San Francisco: Harper/Hazelden. 1987.

Blanchard, Kenneth, Ph.D. and Johnson, Spencer, M.D. **The One Minute Manager.** New York, NY: Wm. Morrow. 1982.

Bradshaw, John. **Bradshaw On: The Family.** Deerfield Beach, FL: Health Communications. 1988.

Drucker, Peter E. **Management: Tasks, Responsibilities, Practices.** New York, NY: Harper & Row. 1973.

Durant, Will and Ariel. **A Dual Autobiography.** New York, NY: Simon & Schuster. 1977.

Gerber, Michael E. **The E Myth.** Cambridge, MA. Ballinger Press. 1985.

Goldratt, Elyahu M. and Cox, Jeff. **The Goal.** Croton-on-Hudson, NY: North River Press. 1987.

Hoffer, Eric. **The True Believer.** New York, NY: Harper & Row. 1951.

Hubbard, L. Ron. **Dianetics.** New York, NY: St. Hill Press. 1950.

Kanter, Rosabeth Moss. **The Change Masters.** New York, NY: Simon & Schuster. 1983.

Keyes, Ken Jr. **Handbook to Higher Consciousness.** Coos Bay, OR: Living Love Publications. 1975.

Kuhn, Thomas S. **The Structure of Scientific Revolutions.** Chicago, IL: University of Chicago Press. 1962.

Lowen, Alexander, M.D. **Narcissism, Denial Of The True Self.** New York, NY: Macmillan Publishing. 1985.

Miller, Keith. **Sin: Overcoming the Ultimate Addiction.** New York, NY: Harper & Row. 1987.

Morgan, James N. and Duncan, Greg J. **The Economics of Personal Choice.** Ann Arbor, MI: University of Michigan Press. 1980.

Naisbitt, John. **Megatrends.** New York, NY: Warner Books. 1982.

Naisbitt, John and Aburdene, Patricia. **Re-inventing the Corporation.** New York, NY: Warner Books. 1985.

Peck, M. Scott, M.D. **People of the Lie.** New York, NY: Simon & Schuster. 1983.

_____ **A Different Drum.** New York, NY: Simon & Schuster. 1987.

Perkins, Rollin and Boyce, Ronald. **Criminal Law and Procedure.** New York, NY: Foundation Press. 1984.

Peters, Tom and Austin, Nancy. **A Passion for Excellence.** New York, NY: Warner Books. 1985.

Peters, Tom and Waterman, Bob. **In Search of Excellence.** New York, NY: Warner Books. 1982.

Pinchott, Gifford III. **Intrapreneuring.** New York, NY: Harper & Row. 1985.

Rand, Ayn. **Atlas Shrugged.** New York, NY: Signet Books. 1957.

Robinson, Bryan E. **Work Addiction.** Deerfield Beach, FL: Health Communications. 1989.

Schaef, Anne Wilson and Fassel, Diane. **Addictive Organizations.** New York, NY: Harper & Row. 1988.

Sheaffer, Robert. **Resentment Against Achievement.** Buffalo, NY: Prometheus Books. 1988.

Terkel, Studs. **Working.** New York, NY: Avon. 1972.

Waterman, Robert H. **The Renewal Factor.** New York, NY: Bantam Books. 1987.

Whitfield, Charles L., M.D. **Healing The Child Within.** Pompano Beach, FL: Health Communications. 1987.

Williams, William J. **General Semantics and the Social Sciences.** New York, NY: Philosophical Library. 1972.

Wilson, Kenneth D. **Prospects for Growth.** New York, NY: Praeger. 1977.

Woititz, Janet. **Home Away From Home.** Pompano Beach, FL: Health Communications. 1987.

# Books from . . .
# Health Communications

*AFTER THE TEARS: Reclaiming The Personal Losses of Childhood*
Jane Middelton-Moz and Lorie Dwinnel
Your lost childhood must be grieved in order for you to recapture your
self-worth and enjoyment of life. This book will show you how.
**ISBN 0-932194-36-2**                                              **$7.95**

*HEALING YOUR SEXUAL SELF*
Janet Woititz
How can you break through the aftermath of sexual abuse and enter into
healthy relationships? Survivors are shown how to recognize the problem
and deal effectively with it.
**ISBN 1-55874-018-X**                                              **$7.95**

*RECOVERY FROM RESCUING*
Jacqueline Castine
Effective psychological and spiritual principles teach you when to take
charge, when to let go, and how to break the cycle of guilt and fear that
keeps you in the responsibility trap. Mind-altering ideas and exercises will
guide you to a more carefree life.
**ISBN 1-55874-016-3**                                              **$7.95**

*ADDICTIVE RELATIONSHIPS: Reclaiming Your Boundaries*
Joy Miller
We have given ourselves away to spouse, lover, children, friends or
parents. By examining where we are, where we want to go and how to get
there, we can reclaim our personal boundaries and the true love of
ourselves.
**ISBN 1-55874-003-1**                                              **$7.95**

*RECOVERY FROM CO-DEPENDENCY:*
*It's Never Too Late To Reclaim Your Childhood*
Laurie Weiss, Jonathan B. Weiss
Having been brought up with life-repressing decisions, the adult child
recognizes something isn't working. This book shows how to change
decisions and live differently and fully.
**ISBN 0-932194-85-0**                                              **$9.95**

---

SHIPPING/HANDLING: All orders shipped UPS unless weight exceeds 200 lbs., special routing is requested, or
delivery territory is outside continental U.S. Orders outside United States shipped either Air Parcel Post or Surface
Parcel Post. Shipping and handling charges apply to all orders shipped whether UPS, Book Rate, Library Rate, Air
or Surface Parcel Post or Common Carrier and will be charged as follows. Orders less than $25.00 in value add
$2.00 minimum. Orders from $25.00 to $50.00 in value (after discount) add $2.50 minimum. Orders greater than
$50.00 in value (after discount) add 6% of value. Orders greater than $25.00 outside United States add 15% of
value. We are not responsible for loss or damage unless material is shipped UPS. Allow 3-5 weeks after receipt of
order for delivery. Prices are subject to change without prior notice.

Enterprise Center, 3201 S.W. 15th Street,
Deerfield Beach, FL 33442
1-800-851-9100
**Health**
**Communications, Inc.**

# Daily Affirmation Books from . . .
# Health Communications

*GENTLE REMINDERS FOR CO-DEPENDENTS: Daily Affirmations*
Mitzi Chandler
With insight and humor, Mitzi Chandler takes the co-dependent and the adult child through the year. Gentle Reminders is for those in recovery who seek to enjoy the miracle each day brings.
**ISBN 1-55874-020-1**                                      **$6.95**

*TIME FOR JOY: Daily Affirmations*
Ruth Fishel
With quotations, thoughts and healing energizing affirmations these daily messages address the fears and imperfections of being human, guiding us through self-acceptance to a tangible peace and the place within where there is *time for joy.*
**ISBN 0-932194-82-6**                                      **$6.95**

*CRY HOPE: Positive Affirmations For Healthy Living*
Jan Veltman
This book gives positive daily affirmations for seekers and those in recovery. Every day is a new adventure, and change is a challenge.
**ISBN 0-932194-74-5**                                      **$6.95**

*SAY YES TO LIFE: Daily Affirmations For Recovery*
Father Leo Booth
These meditations take you through the year day by day with Father Leo Booth, looking for answers and sometimes discovering that there are none. Father Leo tells us, "For the recovering compulsive person God is too important to miss — may you find Him now."
**IBN 0-932194-46-X**                                      **$6.95**

*DAILY AFFIRMATIONS: For Adult Children of Alcoholics*
Rokelle Lerner
Affirmations are a way to discover personal awareness, growth and spiritual potential, and self-regard. Reading this book gives us an opportunity to nurture ourselves, learn who we are and what we want to become.
**ISBN 0-932194-47-3**
**(Little Red Book)**                                      **$6.95**
**(New Cover Edition)**                                     **$6.95**

Enterprise Center, 3201 S.W. 15th Street,
Deerfield Beach, FL 33442
1-800-851-9100

**Health Communications, Inc.**

# Other Books By . . .
## Health Communications

*ADULT CHILDREN OF ALCOHOLICS*
Janet Woititz
Over a year on *The New York Times* Best-Seller list, this book is the primer on Adult Children of Alcoholics.
ISBN 0-932194-15-X                                    $6.95

*STRUGGLE FOR INTIMACY*
Janet Woititz
Another best-seller, this book gives insightful advice on learning to love more fully.
ISBN 0-932194-25-7                                    $6.95

*DAILY AFFIRMATIONS: For Adult Children of Alcoholics*
Rokelle Lerner
These positive affirmations for every day of the year paint a mental picture of your life as you choose it to be.
ISBN 0-932194-27-3                                    $6.95

*CHOICEMAKING: For Co-dependents, Adult Children and Spirituality Seekers* — Sharon Wegscheider-Cruse
This useful book defines the problems and solves them in a positive way.
ISBN 0-932194-26-5                                    $9.95

*LEARNING TO LOVE YOURSELF: Finding Your Self-Worth*
Sharon Wegscheider-Cruse
"Self-worth is a choice, not a birthright," says the author as she shows us how we can choose positive self-esteem.
ISBN 0-932194-39-7                                    $7.95

*BRADSHAW ON: THE FAMILY: A Revolutionary Way of Self-Discovery*
John Bradshaw
The host of the nationally televised series of the same name shows us how families can be healed and individuals can realize full potential.
ISBN 0-932194-54-0                                    $9.95

*HEALING THE CHILD WITHIN:*
*Discovery and Recovery for Adult Children of Dysfunctional Families*
Charles Whitfield
Dr. Whitfield defines, describes and discovers how we can reach our Child Within to heal and nurture our woundedness.
ISBN 0-932194-40-0                                    $8.95

Enterprise Center, 3201 S.W. 15th Street,
Deerfield Beach, FL 33442
1-800-851-9100

Health Communications, Inc.